SIXTIES PRESS ANTHOLOGY OF GREGORY FELLOWS' POETRY

Selected poems by

Martin Bell, Thomas Blackburn, Wayne Brown, Kevin Crossley-Holland, John Heath-Stubbs, Pearse Hutchinson, James Kirkup, Paul Mills, Peter Redgrove, Jon Silkin, Bill Turner and David Wright

Ed[illegible]

Debjani Chatt[illegible]

Sixties Press

2004

SIXTIES PRESS ANTHOLOGY OF GREGORY FELLOWS' POETRY:
Selected poems by Martin Bell, Thomas Blackburn, Wayne Brown, Kevin Crossley-Holland, John Heath-Stubbs, Pearse Hutchinson, James Kirkup, Paul Mills, Peter Redgrove, Jon Silkin, Bill Turner and David Wright

Published by Sixties Press,
89 Connaught Road, Sutton, Surrey, SM1 3PJ, UK
and
27, Sefton Terrace,Leeds LS11 7EL, UK
E-mail: sixtiespress@blueyonder.co.uk
Website: www.sixtiespress.co.uk

ISBN: 0 9529994 8 X
First published 2004

Cover photograph of Leeds

Typesetting by Debjani Chatterjee
Printed by Pauls Press, E44/11, Okhla Industrial Area, Phase II, New Delhi 110020, India

Classification: Poetry

To the children of Class 3A at Wyther Park School, Leeds, 1964 to 1967.

– Barry Tebb

To Roland John and David Tipton, writers and publishers whose support has meant a lot to me.

– Debjani Chatterjee

Contents

TO THE READER

Who *were* the Gregory Poetry Fellows? Most readers may be forgiven for asking this question. It was one that I too had to put to publisher, poet and editor, Barry Tebb, when he invited me to join him in compiling a selection of their poetry. And enlightenment followed. The Gregory Fellows in Poetry were a dozen poets appointed by the University of Leeds during the 1950s, 60s and 70s.

The Gregory Fellowship was a scheme started at this time and named after the printer and art lover Eric Craven Gregory. Scottish-born, Gregory had lived in Bradford and been an arts activist and friend to many a northern artist in the early years of the twentieth century. Henry Moore and Barbara Hepworth could be numbered among his friends. The University of Leeds was chosen for the endowment because it was the nearest university to Bradford. The Gregory Fellowships were always given to talented young or new artists – poets, painters, sculptors and musicians. The scheme enabled its Fellows to live and work in or near the University, with a degree of financial security which allowed them to be innovative and experimental. The fellowships – during their duration – gave them an exhilarating independence and proved a major fillip to their work. They had no formal teaching commitment, but were expected to freely interact with students. Many Gregory Poetry Fellows became role models for students who gained an insight into the practice of writing poetry. The Fellowships were important also in creating a cultural buzz in Yorkshire that drew many an artist from London and elsewhere.

The 1960s had seen Barry Tebb emerge as a working class northern poet who was published in Michael Horovitz's Penguin anthology *Children of Albion* and whose work attracted praise from John Carey in *The New Statesman*. The 1960s – a favourite decade for many a 'flower child', was also a dream decade for Barry Tebb who has named his publishing venture the Sixties Press, and he is certainly knowledgeable about the poetry and the politics of that time. The city of Leeds is his favourite metropolis and looms large – almost like a character in its own right – in Tebb's poetry, fiction and memoirs. Thus a project such as this anthology, is a potent mixture, combining as it does, so many elements that are dear to its publisher's heart. Some of the Gregory Poetry Fellows were writers with a northern connection. Many were also working class poets and 'political' in a way that appeals to Barry – ever a rebel against establishments! They were also poets, for the most part, whom Barry knew personally and, in some cases, had published or befriended. Barry's reminiscences in these pages give a fascinating personal perspective. Also included is a personal introduction by Julia Blackburn to the work of her late father, Thomas Blackburn. It is one writer's moving tribute to another.

A few like Silkin, Redgrove and Crossley-Holland, were also poets whom I had had the pleasure of meeting at readings. Turner had reviewed my first collection in *Poetry Review*, and he and I had once competed – unsuccessfully – for the same post at Sheffield Hallam University. Having made my home in Sheffield, I too am a 'northern' poet, in some sense, and, like such Gregory Fellows as David Wright, James Kirkup and Pearse Hutchinson, I too share an outsider's vision. When I heard that the Gregory Poetry Fellows were: Martin Bell, Thomas Blackburn, Wayne Brown, Kevin Crossley-Holland, John Heath-Stubbs, Pearse Hutchinson, James Kirkup, Paul Mills, Peter Redgrove, Jon Silkin, Bill Turner and David Wright, I realised of course that here were some of the leading poets of their generation. Many were poets whose work I admired, though a few like David Wright, Paul Mills and Pearse Hutchinson, were poets with whose work I was not familiar, and so working on this book has enabled me to make some very welcome discoveries. Sadly, some of the Gregory Fellows are no longer living and some were writers whose published verse is now out of print. But all are poets whose work deserves to be presented to a new generation of poetry readers.

In spite of the common features to which I have drawn attention, the work of the Gregory Poetry Fellows also exhibits a fascinating diversity of cultures, styles, form and content. So how did I answer Barry Tebb's invitation? Naturally I said: "It would be an honour and a delight to join you in this project". I hope that readers will find equal delight within these pages.

Debjani Chatterjee

GREGORY POETRY FELLOWS AS I REMEMBER THEM

While a student at Leeds Training College, I supplemented my course by attending classes at Leeds University run by the then Gregory Fellow in Poetry, Jon Silkin, followed by the sour, dour Scots poet Bill Price Turner and finally Peter Redgrove. I shall never forget the evening I went, with great difficulty, to Guiseley Town Hall to hear him give a reading. The hall was packed and Redgrove had already begun his talk. I pushed my way through the throng of wet raincoats and clouds of cigarette smoke. On the dais Redgrove had survived the chairman's opening remarks and was in full flow.

'A tree in a storm is like a brain in a brain storm',' were the first words I heard. His voice was powerful with an actor's measured delivery, the pitch rising and falling like waves battering a passive shore. His poetry was full of images of raw energy at work in nature, rocks, water-wheels, rainbows and volcanic eruptions against a background of meditations on flowers and quotations from Wittgenstein. He was the perfect catalyst to my nascent creative self. He invited me to join the circle of artists, writers and sculptors which met in The Eldon, the university pub. The writer and critic Douglas Jefferson, an expert on Henry James was also an habitué but though he was on nodding terms with Redgrove, he has his own cronies. I bought all Redgrove's books and went to his weekly creative writing class. Two other members of his class, Jon Glover and Jeffrey Wainbright, have subsequently become reasonably well-known writers and broadcaster. I hated both on sight and the feelings were mutual.

Redgrove was Gregory fellow for three years. In 1966 when Alan Tarling, who ran Poet and Printer Press, invited me to edit a pamphlet anthology of work by contemporary poets, I was delighted to include a selection of Redgrove's verse. Another poet represented in my anthology was Angela Carter who would later become an internationally famous novelist.

Redgrove was followed as Gregory Fellow by the deaf poet David Wright, who belonged to an older and more cosmopolitan group than Redgrove. He had known Dylan Thomas and belonged to the circle of George Barker and David Gascoygne, whose publisher had been David Archer's Parton Press. Just before meeting Wright I wrote a review of an anthology of contemporary verse he had edited for Penguin. The book was full of the work of his friends and I wrote a blistering review that was published in Peace News. Fortunately the review escaped Wright's notice. As a person he was kindness itself but his ideas about poetry seemed very dull. He knew hundreds of anecdotes about the private lives of poets with which he regaled the student literati of Leeds University.

Barry Tebb

Martin Bell

(1918 – 1978)

MARTIN BELL

The last incumbent of the Gregory Fellowship I knew was Martin Bell, a warm, generous alcoholic and a founder-member of the London poetry circle 'The Group'. By the time he came to Leeds alcoholism had too strong a hold on him for poetry to have much chance; nevertheless he was a quite wonderful person to know. When Ted Hughes failed to turn up to give a reading to a Civic Hall packed with hundreds, Bell took the stage and read some of my poems.

Such generosity was typical of this gifted but deeply suffering man. His poems have gone out of favour but this cannot be any more than a temporary eclipse:

For one odd halfpenny, Mosca broke on the rack.
The Senate's liver was hardened with golden wine.
Some money drained to the poor. The young man never came back.
Last heard of, was herding swine, or turned to swine.

('A Prodigal Son for Volpone')

Famous young Rimbaud managed rather better –
Crammed all he could beneath his greedy hide,
Went to Abyssinia, wouldn't write a letter:
Was made into a saint before he died!

('Usumcasane as Poet Maudit')

Of the poets I met in the sixties during what has become known as 'The Leeds Poetry Renaissance', Martin Bell stands out for his giftedness, his humility, his kindness and his ability as a teacher. My memories of him are vague but a sketch of him by George Szirtes, included in the Bloodaxe Completed Poems, seems just right. The meetings I had with him were comparatively few and it is the intense luminous persona of Martin Bell the poet, hunched over his beer, chain-smoking, talking about poetry, always and most intensely talking about poetry, that I remember. His Collected Poems had just come out from Macmillan, a slim hardback with a buff cover which contains the poems he is most remembered for, especially 'El Desdichado' (his 'gothicised version of Nerval'). To me, this is one of the transmutations of greatness from one language into another. Bell's version of line 1: "Je suis le ténébreux-le veuf, l'inconsolé" as "Look for me in the shadow, a bereft one, disconsolate" catches exactly the haunted quality and the precise yet passionate lyricism of the original. De Nerval was very much the poete maudit, suffering bouts of insanity and finally hanging himself on a lamp-post, and perhaps Bell was, too, though less dramatically. He came across to me as being very depressed and constantly trying to alleviate his depression with alcohol. Certainly this problem was serious and no doubt contributed to his continual poverty and his early death, but as Oscar Wilde said – à propos of Ernest Dowson – "You must accept a person for what he is. It is not regrettable that a poet is drunk, but that drunks aren't always poets."

I can't remember Bell either drunk or sober but usually somewhere in-between, always vague about practical matters, usually worried about people he felt he should be helping (he always did help people) but most of all entirely obsessed about poetry to the point of being possessed by it. He would give generously of his time, reading the work of student poets like myself, commenting in detail, making tentative suggestions but most of all encouraging and that, of course, is what poets most need.

Bell's 'poetic voice' is quite at odds with his vague, rather chaotic personality; irony, passion, wit and humour are the qualities I would most readily associate with his writing. The very best are uniquely unforgettable – once read they become part of the reader's personal anthology of great poems. Going through his work, some poems leap off the page:

Noses in books, odd children in good schools
Get praise by being clever. And they sing
Revenge on the fortunate, the easy-going fools;
And think it passing brave to be a king.

King then, but of words only. There's the rub.
Action is suspect and its end uncertain:
Stuck in a job, or browned off in a pub,
Or feted and then stabbed, behind a curtain...
('Usumcasane as Poet Maudit')

Conspicuous consumption? Why, Volpone
Would splash it around as if he could afford it,
Wore himself out for his craft, a genuine phoney,
Who only wanted, gloatingly, to hoard it.

His son had sprung like a mushroom, pale in an alley.
Reluctant, they had to unload the stuff on him.
To cook the accounts, got Mosca back from the galleys –
These lawyers worried that the heir looked dim.
('A Prodigal Son for Volpone')

Barnacled, in tattered pomp, go down
Still firing, battered admirals, still go down
With jutting jaw and tutting tooth and tongue,
Commanding order down cold corridors.

Superbly, O dyspeptic Hamlets,
Pause in the doorway, startle the Fourth Form
With rustlings of impatient inky cloaks –
Time and again you go into your act.
('The Enormous Comics')

Of course there are many, many more but these stand out amongst my favourites. Quite late in life I realised I share Bell's passion for twentieth century French poetry, especially for Pierre Reverdy, of whose work Bell translated about 150 pages, none of which are included in the Bloodaxe *Collected Poems*, but do get a mention in Peter Porter's excellent introduction. The obscure White Knights Press at Reading University brought out the *Reverdy Translations* in 1997 (ISBN 0704901188).

Bell applied to the Arts Council for a bursary to complete his translations and Porter comments, "By the sort of irony common to poets' lives, the money arrived the day after he died." If only the recent neglect of Bell would end and his work be granted the acknowledgement it so richly deserves: in the present climate I very much doubt it.

BT

ABOUT THE POET Martin Bell (1918-1978)

Martin Bell was born in Hampshire in 1918 in a working class family. In the 1930s he was a young member of the Communist Party of Great Britain. From 1939 to 1946 he served in the army with the Royal Engineers. He was a schoolteacher in London from 1956 to 1967.

As founder-member of a poets' group that initially called itself 'The Group' and later became the Writers' Workshop, Bell came to exert an important influence on the work of younger contemporaries like Peter Redgrove and Peter Porter. Peter Porter was later to describe him as "one of the major poets writing in English in the second half of the century".

The 1960s were Bell's best decade. His work was included in the influential anthology, Penguin Modern Poets. Leeds University appointed Bell a Gregory Fellow from 1967 to 1969. From 1968 he was also a part-time lecturer at Leeds College of Art. In 1967 Macmillan brought out his *Collected Poems 1937-1966* – Bell's first full publication and his last. Anthony Burgess commented that "the publication of Martin Bell's *Collected Poems* is as important a literary event as any, not merely [in] this year but in this decade.'

A deeply erudite person, Bell sometimes used the pseudonym Titus Oates. His poems often reflect his concerns with political and social issues, and have a biting edge to them. Inevitably war became a powerful subject for Bell, but he was also capable of writing very delicate love poems. An admirer of French Surrealist poetry, Bell was also an excellent translator of poetry. Music remained an abiding interest and he would write reviews of operas and other musical and theatrical productions.

A drink problem haunted him for most of his life and he died in poverty in Leeds in 1978.

BIBLIOGRAPHY

Penguin Modern Poets: George Baker, Martin Bell, Charles Causley (Penguin, Harmondsworth, 1962).
Collected Poems 1937-1966 (Macmillan, London, 1967).
Complete Poems edited by Peter Porter (Bloodaxe, Newcastle upon Tyne, 1988).

DC

POEMS BY MARTIN BELL

Reasons for Refusal

Busy old lady, charitable tray
Of social emblems: poppies, people's blood –
I must refuse, make you flush pink
Perplexed by abrupt No-thank-you.
Yearly I keep up this small priggishness,
Would wince worse if I wore one.
Make me feel better, fetch a white feather, do.

Everyone has list of dead in war,
Regrets most of them, e.g.

Uncle Cyril; small boy in lace and velvet
With pushing sisters muscling all around him,
And lofty brothers, whiskers and stiff collars;
The youngest was the one who copped it.
My mother showed him to me,
Neat letters high up on the cenotaph
That wedding-caked it up above the park,
And shadowed birds on Isaac Watts' white shoulders.

And father's friends, like Sandy Vincent;
Brushed sandy hair, moustache, and staring eyes.
Kitchener claimed him, but the Southern Railway
Held back my father, made him guilty.
I hated the khaki photograph,
It left a patch on the wallpaper after I took it down.

Others I knew stick in the mind,

And Tony Lister often –
Eyes like holes in foolscap, suffered from piles,
Day after day went sick with constipation
Until they told him he could drive a truck –
Blown up with Second Troop in Greece:
We sang all night once when we were on guard.

And Ken-Gee, our lance-corporal, Christian Scientist –
Everyone liked him, knew that he was good –
Had leg and arm blown off, then died.
Not all were good. Gross Corporal Rowlandson
Fell in the canal, the corrupt Sweet-water,
And rolled there like a log, drunk and drowned.
And I've always been glad of the death of Dick Benjamin,
A foxy urgent dainty ballroom dancer –
Found a new role in military necessity
As R.S.M. He waltzed out on parade
To make himself hated. Really hated, not an act.
He was a proper little porcelain sergeant-major –
The earliest bomb made smithereens:
Coincidence only, several have assured me.

In the school hall was pretty glass
Where prissy light shone through St George –
The highest holiest manhood, he!
And underneath were slain Old Boys
In tasteful lettering on whited slab –
And, each November, Ferdy the Headmaster
Reared himself squat and rolled his eyeballs upward,
Rolled the whole roll-call off an oily tongue,
Remorselessly from A to Z.

Of all the squirmers, Roger Frampton's lips

Most elegantly curled, showed most disgust.
He was a pattern of accomplishments,
And joined the Party first, and left it first,
At OCTU won a prize belt, most improbable,
Was desert-killed in '40, much too soon.

His name should burn right through that monument.

No poppy, thank you.

Senilio Passes, Singing

Solomon Grundy
Bored on Tuesday
Manic on Wednesday
Panic on Thursday
Drunk on Friday
Hung over Saturday
Slept all Sunday
Back to work Monday –
That's the life
For Solomon Grundy.

A Benefit Night at the Opera

The chatter thins, lights dip, and dusty crimson
Curtains start dragging away. Then, at one bound,
A rush of trumpets, ringing brass and vermillion –
The frescoed nymphs sprawl in a sea of sound.

We give our best attention as we must, for
This music is fatal and must be heard.
The glittering fountains vocalise our lust,
The whole brilliant scene sways on to murder.

The idyll interrupted by a cough,
Coloratura soars into a fever.
After the vows, the sibyl shuffles off,
The conspirators' chorus mutter, melt away, leave us

A traitor and his stabbed tyrant, downstage in tears.
Masked revellers are grouping for a wedding.
In stern beat start to life six scarlet halberdiers,
Move with the music, march to a beheading.

Lo! Wild applause proclaims a happy ending.
Vendetta is achieved with clinking swords.
Sheer from the battlements the Diva is descending,
Rash in black velvet and resplendent chords.

It Is the Blight Man Was Born For

I

Don't knock the door. She's not at home
To chat of Crabbe's or Cowper's verse –
Miss Austen's got the curse again,
This time, worse.

Strides over the moors
A recalcitrant Amazon –
Emily Bronte
With the jam-rags on.

Tears are replaced by
Crimson confetti –
Goblins get hold of
Christina Rossetti.

Poor girls,
I bleed for you.

II

Not given a classical treatment
By any English poet –
Not even Shakespeare.

Whose needling bloodied Duncan,
Sullks lost Actium,
Temper cast out Lear?

A Prodigal Son for Volpone

Conspicuous consumption? Why, Volpone
Would splash it around as if he could afford it,
Wore himself out for his craft, a genuine phoney,
Who only wanted, gloatingly, to hoard it.

His son had sprung like a mushroom, pale in an alley.
Reluctant, they had to unload the stuff on him.
To cook the accounts, got Mosca back from the galleys –
These lawyers worried that the heir looked dim.

What was he, now, to do with all this gold?
His father had withered in prison because of it.
Root of all evil, he'd always been told
By scholars who'd brought him up. Get shot of the lot of it.

Gloomy vaults, cram-full roof-high with piles
Of metal and stone and paper shoved into sacks:
A great city's sewer, bustling golden miles
Swollen for carnival. Must give it back,

Somehow get rid of it, be a big spender.
The tradesmen knew of a new purse spilling around.
Not a junk-shop in Venice that wasn't stripped of its splendour,
Not a period-piece, not an objet d'art to be found.

How richly the monde assembled at his parties,
How thickly clustered in slow gilded whirls!
Sensitive businessmen and butch aesthetic hearties,
Senile young statesmen, faint expensive girls.

‘Spend it faster?’ He’d pay on the nail for their answers.
A patron’s deep-waving harvest was quick to be seen.
A sculptor in barbed-wire, a corps of Bulgarian dancers,
Three liberal reviews and a poetry magazine.

Mosca’s smirk broadened. The Foundation showed a profit.
How white and stammering now our Volponetto!
‘G-give it to the city. S-see the poor get some of it.’
He vanished aboard a waiting vaporetto.

For one odd halfpenny, Mosca broke on the rack.
The Senate’s liver was hardened with golden wine.
Some money drained to the poor. The young man never came back.
Last heard of, was herding swine, or turned to swine.

Prospect 1939

(for Campbell Matthews)

‘Life is a journey’ said our education,
And so we packed, although we found it slow.
At twenty-one, left stranded at the station
We’ve heaps of luggage and nowhere to go.

Thomas Blackburn

(1916-1977)

THOMAS BLACKBURN

An early incumbent of the Gregory Fellowship was Thomas Blackburn. His work is almost forgotten or when it is remembered it is usually for the wrong reasons. Like the American poet Theodore Roethke, Blackburn was heavily influenced by Yeats. His early collections published by the Hand and Flower Press, include poems of great imaginative power:

At the woman in the valley
I shook an angry fist
For the damned the summer starlight
And when my lovers kissed
Brought bell, book and candle
And drove them out of town;
But the stars sang; it is you condemn them
Oh pull your own heart down!
('The Heart')

Strangely, it is these poems the critics dismiss and praise instead Blackburn's later rather sour verses about suicide attempts and drinking bouts. Blackburn was before my time in Leeds but those who knew him liked him for his chaotic honesty. On one occasion, totally drunk, he drove his car up the steps of Putney police station. The existential irony of the situation affected even the police, who did not prosecute him. In those long-gone days of the fifties and sixties, even the boys in blue had a sense of humour where poets were concerned.

BT

ABOUT THE POET
Thomas Blackburn (1916-1977)

Thomas (Eliel Fenwick) Blackburn was born in Hensingham, Cumberland, on February 10, 1916. His Anglican priest father was of Mauritian descent and haunted by feelings of sexual guilt. One effect of his racial inferiority complex was to scrub the young Blackburn's face with peroxide to lighten his complexion. In his brilliant autobiographical novel, *A Clip of Steel* (1969), Blackburn was to later describe a childhood of torment.

By his early twenties Blackburn had become an alcoholic and was also addicted to sodium amytal pills. While studying at Cambridge, he suffered a nervous breakdown. After a violent and short-lived marriage, he turned to psychotherapy. Writing became an effective therapy for depression and his student years at the University of Durham were happy ones. He married again and his daughter, the novelist Julia Blackburn, was born in 1948.

Blackburn's first collection of poems, *The Outer Darkness*, was published in 1951. His early work was influenced by that of Yeats. His later poetry has a more relaxed and conversational style. *The Holy Stone* in 1954 brought him deserved critical acclaim. In 1960 he won the Guinness Poetry Prize. *The Price of an Eye* and *Robert Browning* contain his critical work; he wrote a musical drama *The Judas Tree* and several radio plays. *The Feast of the Wolf* (1971) was his final novel.

An inspirational teacher, Blackburn first taught at London's Marylebone Grammar School. Then from 1956 to 1958 he was Gregory Poetry Fellow at the University of Leeds and today a special collection at the university's Brotherton Library houses his literary papers. For many years he taught at the College of St Mark and St John in Chelsea, London, and retired from Whitelands College, London, in 1976.

Blackburn's health deteriorated from 1971 onwards and he died in his beloved Snowdonia in Wales in 1977. His overdose of anti-depressant drugs was widely believed to have been an act of suicide.

SELECT BIBLIOGRAPHY

POETRY COLLECTIONS

The Outer Darkness (Hand & Flower Press, 1951).
The Holy Stone (Hand & Flower Press, 1954).
A Smell of Burning (Bodley Head, 1961).
A Breathing Space (Putnam, 1964).
The Fourth Man (MacGibbon & K, 1971).
The Devil's Kitchen (Bodley Head Children's Books, 1975).
Bread for the Winter Birds: the Last Poems of Thomas Blackburn (Hutchinson, London, 1980).
The Adjacent Kingdom: Collected Last Poems (Peter Owen, 1988).
Poems (Greville Press, 1997).
Selected Poems edited by Julia Blackburn (Carcanet, Manchester, 2001).

OTHER

The Price of an Eye (Greenwood Press, 1961).
Presenting Poetry: A Handbook for English Teachers (Methuen, 1966).
Robert Browning: A Study of His Poetry (Woburn Press, 1967).
A Clip of Steel (MacGibbon & K, 1969).
The Feast of the Wolf (MacGibbon & K, 1971).

DC

INTRODUCTION

When I was a child I used to sit outside my father's study door listening to the sharp hammering of his typewriter and the deep sound of his voice as he muttered and grunted with concentration.

If the door was opened to me, I entered a room that seemed to belong to a different dimension of the world, a place that was thick with the smell of stale cigarette smoke, beer and spirits and thick also with a sense of the urgent energy needed to get the poems written.

Sometimes he would read to me and the magical incantation of the words would roll around my head, as meaningful and as meaningless as music. And because I could remember whole chunks of poetry as easily as he could, we would also sit together side by side and recite things. I can't have been more than eight years old then, but I knew what Othello said when he was about to murder Desdemona and my mind still contains verse after verse of that loud and wild diatribe by Vachel Lindsay which begins:

Fat black bucks in a wine-barrel room
Barrel-house kings with feet unstable
Stamped and roared and hammered on the table …
Beat an empty barrel with the handle of a broom
Hard as they were able,
Boom, boom, BOOM.

Already then, when I was still so young, my father taught me to understand that if you can manage to put your deepest feelings and fears into words, to catch them in a net of metaphor and image, then no matter how vast and terrible they might be, you will come to no harm, you will find a way through to the other side. He said it was all a question of naming and giving shape to the things of darkness.

I think he used his early poetry as a means of keeping the horrors of his childhood at bay and then as he grew older his writing became a pathway which he hoped would eventually lead him towards an acceptance of his own troubled destiny and of the fact of death as an end to life. He was always a tormented man, but he was a brave one too.

He must have become more or less an alcoholic in his early twenties and he never managed to give up the booze for longer than a few months, but the real problem was the pills. During the war he was unthinkingly prescribed a new barbiturate drug called sodium amytal, to calm him down when he got nervous. He took to the drug like a duck to water and over the next thirty years he crunched his way through as much as he could get hold of, at times using three different doctors to provide him with extra prescriptions. The pills combined with the drink to make him increasingly mad, but no one was aware of the cause. When the extent of his addiction was finally understood there was an attempt by various medical psychologists to find a chemical substitute for the amytal. With a wild and slightly demonic glee, he became a willing guinea pig, trying out everything that was on offer: pills for epileptics, pills for schizophrenics and one he was especially proud of because he said it was used to tranquilise rhinoceroses if they needed to be transported from one part of Africa to another. I can see him grinning when he tells me this, grinning like a crocodile.

From when I was still young I understood quite simply that my father was two unconnected people. One of them, whom I loved enormously, was full of talk about gods and animals, ghosts and monsters, full of remembered chunks of people, folk songs, passages from the Bible and devastating but hilarious stories based on his experience of childhood. The other, who scared the life out of me even though he never attacked me directly, was a savage creature who might crawl on all fours, bark like a dog, hit people, scream, or break down windows and doors. I watched wide-eyed as the terrible metamorphosis took place, step by step and irreversible once it had begun. I used to think a wicked magician had put a spell on him and I wondered what on earth could be done to remove it.

Each time again when he emerged from one of these shuffling descents into chaos, he was as shocked as everyone else by what had just happened, full of apology and remorse. And then he would turn to the poetry, using all the strength in his power to make the words come and to bring some light into the darkness.

When I read many of his poems now, it is as though I am hearing them being read to me for the first time; and then, I find myself racing down these corridors of recollection.

Thomas Eliel Fenwick Blackburn was born in Northumberland on 10 February 1916, the second of three children. His mother, Adelaide Fenwick, belonged to that part of the world: she had pale red hair, blue eyes and a fragile white skin that looked as though it might tear if you touched it. His father, Eliel, had come from Mauritius to England when he was in his early twenties. Mauritius, at that time, even more than now, was an island of many races, many variations of skin colour and an intricate hierarchy of prejudice. My grandfather's mother had traces of Indian or African blood in her veins and Eliel was the child who carried this taint most clearly. He was not allowed to go with his brothers and sisters to social events, because the darkness of his skin would shame them all and, when he reached manhood, he was sent to study theology in France and told it would be better for everyone if he never came back. He never did.

In the old family photograph albums, Adelaide's ancestry is represented by endless pale-faced farmers and country squires, their houses and horses , their servants, children and dogs, while Eliel has nothing more to show than one faded image of a wooden house built in the colonial style with a long verandah and the high trees of a tropical forest on all sides. The name *Chamarel* is written underneath. When I was in Mauritius I went to the Chamarel area and looked for the house, but it had disappeared.

Eliel became an English country parson and, eventually, a canon of the church. In his public life he was respected and respectable, even though his parishioners nicknamed him Beliel because he was as dark as the devil. But within the privacy of his home he repeated the pattern of damage that had been done to him. My father had the darkest skin and the wildest nature of the three children and, in an attempt to change and tame him, he was savagely beaten. The skin of his face was rubbed with a mixture of bleach and lemon and when he approached adolescence he was made to sleep first with a bag of stones tied to his back and later with a terrible mousetrap contraption tied to his front – something which my grandfather managed to obtain from a monastery in Mauritius.

My father wrote about all this in his autobiography *A Clip of Steel.* And as a way of trying to understand how so much blame and rage and sadness had bounced down through the generations, I elaborated on what I knew of my father's childhood in a novel I called *The Book of Colour*.

So, this is the story of the nest my father came from. At first he did what was expected of him and went to Cambridge to study law. When I asked him what he had learn there, he told me about the case of the cabin boy who drew the short straw and got eaten by his shipwrecked companions and about a man accused of 'buggering a duck', but most of his Cambridge days were devoted to drinking and the pursuit of wildness. Once he hung from his lip when he fell on the spiked fence he was trying to climb over and he had the scar to prove it. Once he arranged for a gaggle of prostitutes to knock on the door of the provost's room in the middle of the night – and with that he was thrown out.

After Cambridge he had a breakdown and was enrolled as a member of a very genteel madhouse where nobody admitted that anything was wrong, not even the woman who barked all night like a dog.

Then he went to Durham University to study English Literature and there he discovered his love of words and the liberation that words can offer. One of his lecturers gave him a copy of The Complete Angler and taught him the quiet of fly fishing and someone else introduced him to mountaineering. In the delicate business of edging up and across a stretch of almost vertical, almost smooth granite, he found a stillness and a contentment that served him well for many years.

Climbing was the great bond between him and my mother Rosalie and when I was born but was still too young to walk properly they used to put me in a rucksack so that I could go up the rocks with them. By this time my father was teaching at a London grammar school and every holiday was filled with mountains. I can see us setting off into the cold rain of Wales or the Lake District, my father striding ahead, chain smoking, impatient to reach the foot of the rock. Once the climb had started he would relax, smiling and telling jokes as we balanced on tiny precarious ledges.

Until I was seven we lived in London. At night there was a lot of Soho life and drinking to be done, but every morning my father would emerge from his hangover and adopt the ordered discipline of a schoolteacher doing his job. Then in 1955 he became the Gregory Fellow of Poetry at Leeds University and for the next two years nothing was expected of him except to be a poet. As a result the drinking, the pill taking and the roaring dangers increased dramatically.

He separated from my mother when I was eleven and married a very small, intense, difficult and fascinating woman called Peggy Maguire, who knew a great deal about books and people and could drink almost as much as he could.

Then, when he was approaching his fiftieth year, the writing dried up. I remember meeting him and Peggy in Venice. He seemed to have suddenly turned into an old man, walking with his father's doddering step, and looking as if he had been the witness to an unspeakable atrocity. He took me on a tour of the churches and each time we entered one of those dark and sweet smelling buildings he would stumble up the aisle and throw himself face down on the cold stone floor, weeping and asking God to do something.

He moved through this state of grey uncertainty and unhappiness for several years, hardly able to write, losing confidence in his teaching ability and trying out a number of treatments that might have lifted the cloud: ECT which he said he enjoyed; something called deep sleep therapy when you are kept sedated in a dark room for more than a week and have forgotten your own name when you wake; aversion therapy and quantities of new drugs. In the Charing Cross Hospital he went out into the street dressed only in his pyjamas and managed to buy two bottles of gin on tick, bringing them back to share with the other recovering alcoholics in his ward.

Finally, he was introduced to a very wise Jungian analyst who persuaded him that he could try to meet his own past with forgiveness and equanimity. Once that process had started he was able to return gradually to the land of the living and to the joy he found in writing again. But by then his physical strength had been diminished. He no longer had the balance needed for rock climbing and even the walking was curtailed when he fell and broke a rib. Still he took an enraptured pleasure in the beauty of the natural world; in birds, trees, the rising of the sun, the mountains. And he would often emerge out of a strange somnambulant state to talk with sudden clarity and passion about Blake or Yeats, the transmigration of souls, or, his favourite topic, death as the most important event in everyone's life.

Thomas Blackburn died early in the morning of 13 August 1977. I always felt that he would have been very proud of the way he went. He would have boasted how well he had done it, in spite of everything. He would have written a poem commemorating the event.

He died on the day after my twenty-ninth birthday. I remember waking up on that morning, the light streaming clear and grey through the metal-framed windows of the warehouse where I was living and for no particular reason I was filled with laughter and contentment. I remember cleaning an old wooden filing-cabinet that had twenty-nine drawers, one for each year of my life, scrubbing at it with wire wool dipped in bleach and as the harsh smell entered my nostrils it made me think of my father whose face was rubbed with bleach and lemon. There was a phone call from my stepmother a few hours later and she told me he had died. They were at the cottage in Wales.

I had seen him less than a week before. We had arranged to meet at Charing Cross Station and go on to have lunch. He had arrived early and I saw him waiting for me by the station bookshop. He was wearing his favourite pale linen suit and he was swaying gently from side to side, like a tree in the wind. His hair was utterly white and his face was very pale, gleaming like a wax effigy. If he had been a stranger I would not have dared to approach him because he looked so odd, but I knew him well and I was accustomed to his oddness.

He did not see me walking towards him, even though he was gazing in my direction, his chin towards his chest and his eyes raised. When I stood in front of him and said something, I seemed to be waking him out of a trance.

He kissed me on the cheek so that I felt the cold dampness of sweat glistening on his skin. He told me how glad, how very glad he was to see me. He said he had been writing all through the night and the night before, there was such a lot of energy in him, and he had no need of sleep, not any more. He rubbed his hands together as if he was washing them under a tap and said how happy he was, he had never been so happy.

I could see that it was true. After a long time of difficulty when the poems would not come, he was back with them again. The outbreaks of violence had ceased and he had emerged as shaken and exhausted as a newly hatched creature, but with an air of serenity about him. He kept saying how much he looked forward to dying and I think by that he meant that the burden of the past had finally dropped away and now he no longer needed to be afraid of anything.

We set off across the footbridge that leads from the station to the Festival Hall. I walked beside my father and perhaps I had my hand on his arm, although even if I was not touching him I felt as if I was steering him forward over the cracks in the paving stones, over ledges and steps, around the obstruction of lamp posts and people.

We reached the glass-sided restaurant where we planned to have lunch and we managed to buy a plate of something and a glass of something and we sat and faced each other in the bright dazzle of sunlight. We talked about this and that and he produced a poem on a crumpled piece of paper and read it to me, his voice rising loudly above the other voices and above the clattering of knives and forks and spoons on thick white crockery.

When we were making our way back towards the station he sailed full tilt towards the steps that lead from one concrete level to the next and, just before he might have toppled headlong into the abyss, he sat down abruptly, like a toddler who is learning the first rules of walking, without getting hurt. I helped him back to his feet and felt the lumbering weight of him.

He went to Wales the next day, going home to his cottage in the mountains where all the cupboards were full with the memory of his love of climbing: lengths of nylon rope neatly coiled and tied, bunches of thick socks and the big heavy boots he could never bear to throw away, even when the leather was so gnarled and split they looked like the relics of old saints.

The cottage was one of a row of four mean little houses that seemed to have been plucked from the depths of a crowded industrial town and dumped here at the end of a narrow road, far away from everything except for the sound of the sheep bleating. The cinema-red carpets were stained with mould, the grey slate floors were always damp and cold and a crystalline fungus had pushed its way through successive layers of gloss paint in the kitchen and outside privy. But looking out from the sitting room window or, better still, from one of the upstairs bedrooms, you were confronted with the wonderful sweep of a green valley rushing into the distance, framed by the steep outline of the mountain called Knicht on one side and the rounded contour of the mountain called Moelwyn Mawr on the other.

In the cottage, my father continued to feel very happy and to look forward to dying. For several days he only slept if he happened to doze in one of the huge collapsing armchairs. He kept on writing, urgently, feverishly, in a red notebook and a blue notebook and another blue notebook, the words swarming like insects over the pages, the letters changing size and shape, now brazen with loops and curves, now crammed together in a huddled knot. He wrote about each new dawn as it broke across the valley. He wrote about his love for the mountains, about the magpies hopping outside the window – one for sorrow, two for joy – and he wrote that he knew now that he had chosen his own particular and difficult destiny.

His wife and his brother-in-law had no way of communicating with him; they could only watch and wait. They were woken up each morning by the smell of cooking as he prepared a terrible breakfast of sweet black instant coffee and eggs and bacon fried in a wobbly pan until the little kitchen was invaded by a blue smoke which permeated the whole house.

The notebooks were filled with poems, some of which are included here. He also wrote several letters. The last was to his brother. It went on for page after page, the thoughts spinning and turning. He finished with the words, 'Now having worked from dawn to dusk and dawn again, I must go and lie in a horizontal position and sleep long and deep. Goodnight.'

Then he made his way up the stairs and into one of the bedrooms with its fine view of the valley and, just as he was getting into bed, he was knocked to the ground by a violent cerebral haemorrhage. My stepmother said he cried out briefly as he fell and when she came to him she could see by the early morning light that he was dead.

JULIA BLACKBURN

POEMS BY THOMAS BLACKBURN

The Lucky Marriage

I often wonder as the fairy-story
Tells how the little goose-girl found her prince,
Or of the widowed queen who stopped her carriage
And threw a rose down to the gangling dunce,
What is the meaning of this lucky marriage
Which lasts forever, it is often said,
Because I know too well such consummation
Is not a question of a double bed,
Or of the wedding bells and royal procession
With twenty major-domos at its head.

At least its bride and groom must be rejected,
The fairy godmother will only call
On Cinders scrubbing tiles beside the chimney
While her proud sisters foot it at the ball;
From all but the last son without a birthright
The beggarwoman hordes her magic seed.
Well, if they'd had the good luck of their siblings
And found occasion kinder to their need,
They would have spent their breath on natural pleasures
And had no time for murmurs in the night:
They heard because they were condemned to silence,
And learnt to see because they had no light.

I mean the elder son and cherished sister
Know but the surface of each common day;
It takes the cunning eye of the rejected
To dip beneath that skin of shadow-play

And come into the meaning of a landscape.
I think that every bird and casual stone
Are syllables thrust down from some broad language
That we must ravel out and make our own.
Yet who is ever turned towards that journey
Till deprivations riddle through the heart?
And so I praise the goose-girl and the scullion
Beside a midden or a refuse cart.

And yet all images for this completion
Somehow bypass its real ghostliness
Which can't be measured by a sweating finger,
Or any salt and carnal nakedness.
Although two heads upon a single pillow
May be the metaphor that serves it best,
No lying down within a single moment
Will give the outward going any rest;
It's only when we reach beyond our pronouns
And come into ourselves that we are blest.
Is this the meaning of the lucky marriage
Which lasts forever, it is often said,
Between the goose-girl and the kitchen servant,
Who have no wedding ring or mutual bed?

The Villain

The villain of the play is always absent;
Though every generation drapes its stage
With gaudy Lucifers, some knowing smile
Wipes clean the backcloth for a later age
To deck with targets of a brisker style
For the more recent needles of our rage;
It seems we were mistaken all the while.

Children say any marshlight stole their peace
And grope for culprits till they understand
No slaughtered mouse can make the torment cease,
Or rummaged gutter yield their promised land.
The point is that the torment must increase
Until its causes nestle to the hand,
Though children swear a marshlight stole their peace.

That peace is where the movement is our own;
I mean there is no place in which to stay
And deck with photographs that make a home,
Stone walls to keep the exodus at bay;
Because the going out is situation
In every perished moment of our day
And only minerals have a single station;
I mean there is no place in which to stay.

To whom do beggars post when wishes ride
But the first woman? There's no gentleman
Would leave that old Dutch for another bride.
Who moved the stubborn digit to his plan
And placed a sword of omen at her side?
Is he the rat within the palace wall?
'We seek blue moon,' the little children cried.
Well, with no prompting they'd not seek at all.
To whom do beggars post when wishes ride?

I'm sure that going out was not our choosing;
The lines were written then the play began
In which the tragic fool must gain by loosing
Wherever he's the self-sufficient man.

It seems we are the villain's destination;
You know the way a long keen sword-blade slips
Between true lovers and their consummation
And strikes the heart-shaped chalice from our lips.
We'd set up home; but he insists on leaving
The ruined cottage that our love restored,
Chalks up 'For Sale' and then despite our grieving
Marts the whole place for straw and moves abroad.

The villain of the play is always absent;
But when the final curtain rumbles down
I sometimes think the action may unfold
Beyond the dead King and his witless clown.
There is another story to be told.
The villain of the play is always absent
Until the final curtain rumbles down.

No Single Station

No single station of the globe
Can rest the urgency of love,
Whose true vocation must exceed
All pastures where its children feed.
Transcending in one breathless act
The possibilities of fact,
We learn no mortal creature is
The end of love's intensities.
And thus within our nuptial play
The blinding cloths are torn away,
Releasing on both noon and night
The reaches of an inward sight,
Until our disillusions bless
A vision born of nakedness.

The Younger Son

(for G Wilson Knight)

The crowns return to dust, the sweetmeats vanish,
When the third son with his deliberate eye
Looks coldly through the banquet and the bauble
And proves the witch's palace is a lie.
But always, as in solitude and silence
He takes his stick and buckles on his load,
He sees the two grey dolmens of his brothers
Beside the deprivation of the road.

They did not understand the glare and music
To which they spurred their horses through the night
Were not the goal itself, but only beacons
To keep their passion of the quest alight,
And when some gaudy woman of the palace
Threw down her handkerchief and made sweet moan,
Each clattered up the stairs into her bedroom
And on the stroke of midnight turned to stone.

The journey was itself their occupation
And not some minion of a torchlit hall;
Of course the heart must beat, the pulses quicken
Or there's no road or journeying at all,
But still a certain irony is needed.
I mean that when the princess is awake,
The younger son who sought her in the forest
And plucked her jewel from the haunted lake
Is quick to guess, there, at the crux of passion,
The journey was not merely for a bride,
But some new clarity that rinsed his nature
When he cut through the brambles to her side.

But only his obedience to the language
Of birds and suppliant fishes by the way
Can yield the hero that momentous secret
Which topples giants headlong to the clay.
The elder sons exchange such night time murmurs
For the new guide-book of some master hand,
Then take the hopeless turning at the cross-roads
And walk their lives out in a waste of sand.

Now, by the monolith before the castle,
The third son hears the slug-horn fade and die,
Then gasps at the great bastion of those shoulders
A league above him in the punished sky.
No wonder as earth shook and giant fingers
Groped slowly inward through the forest trees,
His brothers, lost within their own phantasma,
Went headlong into blindness on their knees.

For saplings bend, rocks split, the grass is ravished,
When to the urgent summons of that horn
Some passion of the heart rears out of silence
To drench our landscape with its furious dawn.
Then only those whom birds and fish have tutored
Can hold their upright posture by the stone,
Because they know the energies that nourish
The passion of the monster are their own.
This is the younger son's most precious secret;
And may we also hear the trapped bird cry
And be rewarded by a naked vision
When our appalling manias shake the sky.

Oedipus

His shadow monstrous on the palace wall.
That swollen boy, fresh from his mother's arms,
The odour of her body on his palms,
Moves to the eyeless horror of the hall.

And with what certainty The Revelation
Gropes for the sage's lips; words whine and bark
Out of that crumpled linen in the dark
To name the extremity of violation.

How should he not but tremble as the world
Contracts about him to his mother's room,
Red-curtains, stifling; in the fire-lit gloom
His swollen manhood on her bed is curled.

Then up and blind him, hands, pull blackness down
And let this woman on the strangling cord,
Hang in the rich embroidery of her gown;
Then up and blind him, pull the blackness down.

But as he stumbles to the desert sands,
Bleeding and helpless as the newly born,
His daughters leading him with childish hands,
I see beyond all words his future shape,
Its feet upon the carcass of the ape
And round its mighty head, prophetic birds.

Trewarmett

for Julia Blackburn

Darkness, feathers are shed;
These birds are gathered back
By the enormous hand.
That cast them at dawn seaward
In crumbs of living bread
To their forefathering rock.

Piercing the lens of a wave,
From the beat of it and the swell,
The feathered life they have
Is indivisible,
As from the undertow
And skin of a nervous sca
Fish and themselves also
They reap perpetually.
Being clothed, and without a seam,
In the pouring waters they thread,
How can they miss their aim,
By the loose surge targeted
Forever towards their home?

Darkness, feathers are shed;
From this bird-whitened stone,
I watch a cormorant pluck
Life from a nervous sea,
With a moon behind my back,
Conscious of God knows what
Anxious irrelevance
As these birds swim in the eye
Of the green circumstance
From which I am undone
By my duplicity.

A Small Keen Wind

My wife, for six months now in sinister
Tones, has muttered incessantly about divorce,
And, since of the woman I'm fond, this dark chatter
Is painful as well as a bit monotonous.
Still, marvel one must, when she fishes out of that trunk,
Like rags, my shadier deeds for all to see
With 'This you did when sober, and that when drunk',
The dirty linen I simply cannot drop,
Since 'Thomas Blackburn 'is stitched by the laundry mark.
So I gather the things and say 'Yes, these are mine;
Though some cleaner items are not upon your list',
Then walk with my bundle of rags to another room
Since I will not play the role of delinquent ghost
And be folded up by guilt in the crook of an arm.
I saw tonight – walking to cool the mind –
A little moonshine on a garden wall
And as I brooded, felt a small, keen winde
Stroll from the Arctic at its own sweet will.

Wayne Brown

(b. 1944)

ABOUT THE POET Wayne Brown (b. 1944)

Wayne Brown was born in Port of Spain, Trinidad on 18th July 1944 and has divided most of his life between Trinidad and Jamaica. Always interested in writing, he became a staff journalist for *The Trinidad Guardian* from 1963 to 1965. In 1965 he enrolled on a BA (honours) course in English Literature at the University of the West Indies in Kingston, Jamaica. After graduation, he was briefly a school teacher in Jamaica, before returning to Trinidad to teach from 1970 to 1971. He combined teaching with work as an art critic for *The Trinidad Guardian.*

In 1968, the year of his graduation, Wayne Brown married Megan Hopkyn-Rees and also won the Jamaican Independence Festival Poetry Prize. His poems were appearing regularly in Caribbean journals and Brown was still in his twenties when his collection *On the Coast* appeared from a major London publisher, André Deutsch. Dedicated to Derek Walcott, the book also contains individual poems for the Jamaican poets Dennis Scott, Anthony McNeill and Mervyn Morris. This impressive debut collection won the Commonwealth Poetry Prize.

Seventeen years later Brown's second poetry collection *Voyages* was published by a small Trinidadian press. In the years between, he wrote a biography of the Jamaican sculptress, Edna Manley, and edited Derek Walcott's *Selected Poetry.*

From 1974 to 1976 Wayne Brown was inspiring British students as a Gregory Fellow in Poetry at the University of Leeds. During this time he edited *21 Years of Poetry and Audience* for the university's English Department; this was a commemorative anthology of poems drawn from its long-running poetry journal, containing work by the major British poets of the previous two decades, from Dylan Thomas to Ted Hughes.

Brown has been a Fulbright Scholar in the USA, and a Fellow of Yaddo, MacDowell, The Virginia Center for the Creative Arts, and the Rockefeller Foundation's Lake Como scholar's retreat in Bellagio. He has taught English Literature at the University of the West Indies and tutored on the MFA creative writing programme of Lesley University in Cambridge, Massachusetts. Brown has written two collections of stories and reminiscence, *The Child of the Sea* (1990) and *Landscape with Heron* (2000). He has also edited several books for Jamaica Observer Publishers and The Mill Press, and produced some 3000 editions of his column 'In Our Time' in Trinidad and Jamaica. Currently Brown is editor-producer of The Literary Arts Supplement of the *Sunday Observer*, tutor at UWI's school of journalism, and founder-tutor of the Observer Creative Writing Workshop.

Brown's poetry celebrates the landscape and the seascape of the Caribbean. It can also be political and ironic when commenting on the postcolonial Caribbean scene. His output of poetry, though relatively small, is of a consistently high quality. Anne Cluysenaar has said "Wayne Brown is outstanding amongst West Indian poets".

SELECT BIBLIOGRAPHY

POETRY COLLECTIONS

On the Coast (André Deutsch, London, 1973).
Voyages (Inprint Caribbean, Port of Spain, Trinidad, 1989).

OTHER

Edna Manley: The Private Years 1900-1938 (André Deutsch, 1976).
21 Years of Poetry and Audience, edited with Tom Wharton (Aquila, Solihull, Warwickshire, 1976).
The Child of the Sea: Stories and Remembrances (Inprint Caribbean, 1990).
Editor, *Selected Poetry of Derek Walcott* (Heinemann Caribbean,

1981).
Editor, *The Love Parting and Other Poems* by Jullia Rypinski (The Mill Press, Jamaica, 1999).
Landscape with Heron (Observer Literary Books, 2000).
Editor, *Freeing Her Hands to Clap* by Delores Gauntlett (Jamaica Observer Publishers, 2001).
Editor, *The Balm of Dusk Lilies* by Frances Coke (Jamaica Observer Publishers, 2001).
Editor, *In the Kingdom of Light: Collected Poems* by M G Smith (The Mill Press, 2003).

DC

POEMS BY WAYNE BROWN

Cat Poem

1
In the Beginning
The cat
Watched for a while from the edge of the world.
On the seventh day
It moved in,
Like your dead neighbour's, casually.

2
Adam and cowering Eve
Felt the eyes watching and vainly tried
To cover their privates: but all that night
The cats streamed in through the garden gate.

3
Noah, while the others stood round in pairs,
Reached forward to greet the bird with the branch.
But the cat killed it
With one slap.

4
The white cat's eyelids slide shut.
The Alps are completely snowed under.

5
Antony dead, the woman dead,
Rome hushed and waiting, emptily –
The cat stalked out of the palace.

6
O daughters of Africa,
Your warriors are slain.
The night is a black cat
With yellow eyes.

7
Arthur, cantering back to the castle
After an exhausting peace,
Noticed a cat trapped halfway
Up a tree-trunk.

8
Whether what woke you sounded like
A dropped nail-file,
Or a bottle,
Or the night of the sailors, think:
The cat's in your garbage,
Woman.

9
Five hundred Viet Cong captured.
Race riots erupt in Atlanta.
Glancing sideways, hurriedly crossing the lit street,
The cat loped off
Down an alley.

10
Dying in his sleep, one step past death,
Heard the love-scream of cats and made
A terrible effort to sit up.

11
The morning after the bomb
Was dropped, I woke early.
Silence past stillness, the city in ruins –
My hand touched fur and the cat purred.

On the Coast

'... words which love had hoped to use,
Erased with the surf's pages.'
Derek Walcott, ISLANDS

I
The light founders. Rain puckers the ocean.
I see a small town, found, then forgotten,
rusting in silence by a sea's edge
where liners no longer come.

You came to me here, bewildered girl,
your body warm and heavy with sleep.
Your eyes were calamitous waters.
How grave were your admonitions!

Later you spoke to me quietly,
as at a distance or under rain
the sea nuzzles her sandspit.
You were beautiful, and I loved you.

Will you never be home again?

II

The warehouse on the waterfront
is empty tonight. The ocean shines.
Moon, it is a winter moon,
a moth's wing netted in cloud.

Why do I sit up these late nights
barefooted on a broken pier?
I never saw galleons enter the moon,
nor the great house that burned on the hill,

And the unpunctual fisherman
who came out of nowhere suddenly
rounding the point on long oars,
had nothing to say to me.

Night, I am getting nowhere.
Island girl, I am scared, don't leave me.

III

Across the bay the streetlamps stare
like amber intersections, and aimlessly
a tree's
shadow splashes the seawall.

The surf turns its pages on dark sand,
the dark boats slip by me as by a lantern,
darkness devours the voices,

And I am an orphaned islander,
on a sandspit of memory,
in a winter
of bays. I have no home.

The Tourists

'The sun works for the Tourist Board'
was a bad joke. But now each noon
the sun toils like a fisherman
with a hard tide to beat,
or a farmer whose wife will drop soon.

And in truth the beach is replete
with strangers. Each one arranges
tenderly his limbs for those brass rays
as a woman, testing each pose, changes
into nothing for her lover's gaze.

The natives mind their own business.
Some blond types are at it again.
An English anthropologist
praises the texture of a seine.
The sea's heard it all before.

A scene from a tourist
brochure. Under that sun
all is languid, and those who come
will find nothing unusual, not
one gesture or motion overdone.

But for one parrot-fish which turns
grave somersaults on the stainless steel
spear that's just usurped its dim
purpose; which was to swim
as usual through blue air, in silence, like the sun.

Sing Willow

(for Megan)

To this island, urged by the pushing
sea, you, strumpet, were early borne.
Your tall nursemaids
whispered obscenities like hummingbirds

at your quick ear and vanished, leaving you
stripping a butterfly, practising words.
Combers for dialogue grew in your side.

Frowning, bared, upon cyclical tides
you learnt from the start
the pure myth of choice:
you built your child's castles of smooth white stones.

One day the trickle of bad men began.
You giggled and ran
backward through bush to the waterfall, where,
crouched like a carving, each hand to a breast,
you suffered black towering dreams like cliffs

in the whitening moon, a big girl growing…

Each morning the sun between your thighs
unravelled the beach, that diary where
you numbered the hulks shipwrecked among your castles.
So you became your island.

That when, on a low rusting dawn,
one sea-blackened sailor, ram on the wind,
came tacking and cresting towards your delta,
to what minstrelsy of nursemaid, comber and fall.

Did your tides draw him on, in clear light,
to what fabulous landfall, and
you, Desdemon,
the rivermouth silting after his wake, like history?

Drought

The woman is barren. And the blackbirds
Have had a hard time this year with the drought
And fallen like moths to the field's floor.

The woman is barren. And the city,
Crawling south like an oil-slick,
Will soon be around her ankles.

So she sings: 'Will you marry me?
I will go searching under many flat stones
For moisture of the departed rains.'

Sings, 'O World, will you marry me?'

The riverbed's dried up completely, the lizards
Have taken to the trees, to the high branches.
The cane rolls westwards, burning, burning.

In the sunset of her time, in the ploughed crater
Where the woman like a frail apostrophe
Dances palely each evening

Among the fallen blackbirds.

Light and Shade

1
These potted plants
grow like your child
unfurling, all on the light's side

2
Bookshelves: their lining
of memories, leaning
together or apart
like small plantations:

A bandstand in the forest
which the musicians left
at sunset, leaving their music

And a brown girl trapped
in the moon's net.

3
I am ten years older
and each year still
besotted by sunlight.

4
This poem is a wall.
Or maybe a string

Of mountains, out of whose blue haze
may yet come (if I am patiently dumb)

Hannibal, swaying widely as his elephant sways.

Kevin Crossley-Holland

(b. 1941)

ABOUT THE POET
Kevin Crossley-Holland (b. 1941)

Kevin (John William) Crossley-Holland was born in Buckinghamshire, on February 7, 1941. He attended Bryanston School and St Edmund Hall, Oxford, graduating in English Language and Literature.

He worked as an editor for Macmillan publishers from 1962 to 1971. Many early books for children, like *Havelok the Dane* and *The Green Children*, were published by this company. Long interested in Anglo-Saxon studies, Crossley-Holland is a distinguished translator of Old English who has translated *The Battle of Maldon and Other Old English Poems*, *Beouwulf* and *Storm and Other Old English Riddles* for Macmillan. By the 1970s Crossley-Holland was well-known as a best-selling writer of children's fiction. Recently his *The Seeing Stone* (2000) has won several prizes, including the Guardian Children's Fiction Award, and been translated into twenty-one languages. Crossley-Holland has collaborated with composers and written libretti for three operas. He has co-written (with Ivan Cutting) a play about the birth of East Anglia, *The Wuffings*, produced by Eastern Angles in 1997.

Along with retellings of Norse myths, British folktales and novels for children, Crossley-Holland also has fine poetry collections. Outposts published *On Approval* in 1961 and Enitharmon has brought out recent ones, including a *Selected Poems* in 2001.

Leeds University appointed him as Gregory Fellow in Poetry (1969 to 1971) and its Brotherton Collection has acquired his literary archive. In 1972 he joined the BBC as a Talks Producer. He returned to publishing as Editorial Director of Victor Gollancz from 1972 to 1977. He often lectures abroad for the British Council. He has held prestigious academic posts at: the University of Regensburg, St Olaf College, Minnesota, and the University of St Thomas, Minnesota. A patron of the Society for Storytelling and a Fellow of the Royal Society of Literature, he became, in 2001, an Honorary Fellow of St Edmund Hall, Oxford.

Married to a Minnesotan wife, Crossley-Holland has two sons and two daughters. He lives on the north Norfolk coast in East Anglia.

SELECT BIBLIOGRAPHY

POETRY COLLECTIONS

On Approval (Outposts, London, 1961).
My Son (Turret, London, 1966).
Norfolk Poems with photos by J Hedgecoe (Academy Editions, 1970).
More Than I Am (Steam Press, London, 1971).
The Rain-Giver (Deutsch, London, 1972).
Petal and Stone (Sceptre Press, Knotting, Bedfordshire, 1975).
The Dream-House (Deutsch, London, 1976).
Between My Father and My Son (Black Willow, Minncapolis, 1982).
New and Selected Poems 1965-1990 (Hutchinson, 1991).
Eleanor's Advent (Old Stile, 1992).
The Language of Yes (Enitharmon Press, 1996).
Poems from East Anglia (Enitharmon Press, 1997).
Selected Poems (Enitharmon Press, 2001).

OTHER

Translator, *Beowulf* (Macmillan, 1968).
Translator, *Storm and Other Old English Riddles* (Macmillan, 1970).
Editor, with Patricia Beer, *New Poetry 2* (Arts Council, London, 1976).
Editor, *The Faber Book of Northern Legends* (Faber, London, 1977).
The Norse Myths (Andre Deutsch, London, 1980).
British Folk Tales (Orchard, 1987).
The Seeing Stone (Orion, 2000).
Editor, with L Sail, *The New Exeter Book of Riddles* (Enitharmon, 1999).

DC

POEMS BY KEVIN CROSSLEY-HOLLAND

A Dream of a Meeting

Rooted I watch, watch the girl
approach in a street hedged with
poppies, trembling, hollyhocks
nodding their acquiescence.
There are always hollyhocks.
Gravely she walks with perfect
equilibrium; daylight
sleepwalker, ashen-faced,
she looms towards this meeting
she knows nothing of.
                                        I strain
my eyes to see her features
as a sculptor searches stone,
finding there correlatives
of his own huge passion.
Her face is a lily spathe
with no blemish, and her hair,
moon-pale, falls out behind her.
Green-sheathed she grows now, grows
towards me.
                        And then I see
she is only eight, maybe
nine. A cigarette, unlit,
waits in her mouth. Still rooted,
I frown like the puritan
I am, I still partly am.
No, not a cigarette, no,
it is a thermometer

jammed under her tongue; the sun
angles off it.
                    And she comes
so very close now, at last
she sees me, hands outstretched.
Her eyes are child's marbles
as she gives me the slender,
gleaming stem of glass, passes
by me; and she does not even
change her metronomic pace.
The sap surges within me,
I look for the mercury:
it is all, all in the bulb,
in the bulb this summer day.
Rooted, I ache. And the girl
goes on gravely. Unknowing,
she brushes trembling poppies
with her bare legs; their scarlet
petals spill like drops of blood.
And all the hollyhocks nod.

Dusk, Burnham-Overy-Staithe

The blue hour ends, this world
floats on a great stillness.

I only guess where marsh
finishes and sky begins,

each grows out of the other.
In the creek a slip

of water gleams. Rowboats
bob and swing above the mud,

the barnacled and broken
ribs of Old Stoker's boat.

A wedge of gulls rustles
overhead, and for a moment

the water notices them.
Such calm is some prelude.

Then across the marsh it comes,
the sound as of an endless

train in a distant cutting,
the god working his way back,

butting and shunting,
reclaiming his territory.

This world's his soundbox now;
in the stillness he still moves.

Anything could happen.

Confessional

I come once more to this terrible place;
As it was it is, each stone and each face

Unchanged, making an index of the change
In me. Everything here was arranged

Long ago; the wind, raking from the north,
Saw to that and sees to it. In the hearth

Coals glow and the ash flies early and late;
Every face is ruckled, sands corrugate;

Inland, those superstitious hawthorn trees
Strain away from the wind and heckled seas.

Yet I come. Here alone I cannot sham.
The place insists that I know who I am.

Elemental trinity – earth, air, sea –
Harshly advocate my humility;

You are bigoted, over ambitious,
You are proud, you salute the meretricious.

Then I have altered this much with the years:
That I need more to admit my errors,

From fear, and a longing not to be blind;
So I am scoured by the unchanging wind,

And rid again of some superfluity
By that force uninterested in me.

And I can go, prepared for the possible;
Dream and bone set out from the confessional.

The Wall

I am a desolate wall, accumulator of lichen.
Men made me with flint chippings and, fickle as always,
ignored me; time did not ignore them.
My business is to divide things: the green ribbons
of grass from the streams of macadam; the kitchen gardens
from the marsh acres, garish with sea-lavender;
the copses of ilex and pine from the North Sea,
the bludgeoning waves of salt water where seabirds play.
I stand grey under the East Anglian sky,
glint when the occasional sun opens its eye.

My business is to divide things, my duty to protect.
I am unrepaired; men neglect me at their own risk.
Time takes me in mouthfuls; the teeth of the frost
bit into my body here; here my mortar crumbles;
the wind rubs salt into every wound.
Elsewhere I am overgrown with insidious ivy;
it wound its arms around me only to strangle me.

Relentless, the sea rolls down from the Pole.
It levelled the dunes last year, removed the marram grass,
clashed its steel cymbals over the marsh and macadam.
It attacked me and undermined me; I sway
like a drunkard now; yet it could not gash me
with its gleaming scythes; it was not strong enough.
I stand, sad, and stare at all this estate,
the lawns, the kitchen gardens, copses garrulous
in the wind. I carefully listen, listen and wait
for the fierce outsider to force his way in.

A Lindisfarne Tombstone

for Eric Elstob

1
Norsemen storm the cells:

The hive ablaze; sluice of blood,
Garnet-bright, under sword and axe;
The golden comb iron reaps;
A knot of monks drone Pax Pax
By candles' light; wax weeps.

A furore Normanorum, libera nos, Domine.

2
Two monks crooked in prayer:

Cuthbert incorrupt and unscathed;
A good haul from Bee Hill;
Quick requital for slaughter;
Freedom from shadows still
Shrithing over the minds' water.

A furore Normanorum, libera nos, Domine.

Vision

Watch me if you want to.
I'm as shifty as a daddy-long-legs
on a polished pane.
You are where I was
and you will never catch me.

Why do you never tire of me?
Is it simply that I am
always beyond you,
all but indiscernible,
air trembling before rain?

I am your pursuit,
your thirst, your one thought;
only the mirage
that only will refresh you.
Watch me (if you want to).

Woman Sorting Redcurrants

Her back is still straight but
her eyes are bleeding.
Through the honeysuckle trellis
where she sits and sorts
swarm the domestic atrocities.

Again and again she tells
their names and their names
do not control them …

This sweetness is almost
unendurable. With her pale
wrist she dabs at her eyes;
unheard, the perfect drops
patter into the kitchen chalice.

John Heath-Stubbs
(b. 1918)

ABOUT THE POET John Heath-Stubbs (b. 1918)

John Francis Alexander Heath-Stubbs was born in London on July 9, 1918. His childhood in rural Hampshire and the Isle of Wight gave him a life-long love of nature and natural history. He was educated at Bembridge School, Worcester College for the Blind, and Queen's College, Oxford. At Oxford he was influenced by the teaching of C S Lewis and Charles Williams, and forged strong friendships with poets who were his fellow-students – Sidney Keyes, William Bell and Drummond Allison. He graduated with English (honours) in 1942.

Heath-Stubbs became first a teacher at Hall School in Hampstead, London, from 1944 to 1945; and then an editorial assistant at Hutchinson and Company from 1045 to 1946. From 1952 to 1955 he was appointed Gregory Poetry Fellow at the University of Leeds. After this he served as Visiting Professor of English at the University of Alexandria in Egypt (1955 to 1958) and at the University of Michigan, Ann Arbor (1960 to 1961). From 1963 to 1972 Heath-Stubbs taught English at the College of St Mark and St John in London.

A much-loved teacher, Heath-Stubbs has also written a number of critical studies and edited anthologies of work by past and contemporary poets. He is also a distinguished translator, especially of Persian poetry. A most co-operative and friendly person, Heath-Stubbs has often collaborated with other editors and translators. His own output of poetry is large and impressive for its technical skill and panoramic range of subject matter.

Heath-Stubbs has won many awards for his writing, including an Arts Council of England bursary in 1965, the prestigious Queen's Gold Medal for Poetry in 1974, and the Oscar Williams-Jean Derwood Award in 1978. He is a Fellow of the Royal Society of Literature. Leeds University's Brotherton Library houses his literary papers in a special collection.

A *Times Literary Supplement* reviewer has commented that: "His poetry is formidable, amiable, hugely intelligent and sacramental."

SELECT BIBLIOGRAPHY

POETRY COLLECTIONS

Wounded Thammuz (Routledge, London, 1942).
Satires and Epigrams (Turret, London, 1968).
Penguin Modern Poets 20, with F T Prince and Stephen Spender (Penguin, London, 1971).
A Parliament of Birds (Chatto and Windus, London, 1975).
The Watchman's Flute (Carcanet, Manchester, 1978).
The Mouse, the Bird and the Sausage (Ceolfrith Press, Sunderland, 1978).
Naming the Beasts (Carcanet, 1982).
Cats Parnassus (Hearing Eye, London, 1987).
Collected Poems 1943-1987 (Carcanet, 1988).
Selected Poems (Carcanet, 1990).
Sweetapple Earth (Carcanet, 1993).
Galileo's Salad (Carcanet, 1996).
The Sound of Light (Carcanet, 1999).
The Return of the Cranes (Carcanet, 2002)).

OTHER

The Darkling Plain: A Study of the Later Fortunes of Romanticism in English Poetry from George Darley to W B Yeats (Eyre and Spottiswoode, London, 1950).

Charles Williams (Longman, London, 1955).
Translator, with Peter Avery, *Thirty Poems of Hafiz of Shiraz* (Murray, London, 1955).
Helen in Egypt and Other Plays (Oxford University Press, 1958).
Translator, with Iris Origo, *Selected Poetry and Prose* by Giacomo Leopardi (Oxford University Press, 1966).
Editor, *Selected Poems of Alexander Pope* (Heinemann, London, 1964).
The Verse Satire (Oxford University Press, 1969).
The Ode (Oxford University Press, 1969).
The Pastoral (Oxford University Press, 1969).
Editor, with Martin Green, *Homage to George Barker on His 60th Birthday* (Martin Brian and O'Keeffe, London, 1973).
Editor, with David Wright, *The Faber Book of Twentieth Century Verse* (Faber & Faber, London, 1975).
Translator, with Shafik Megally, *Dust and Carnations: Traditional Funeral Chants and Wedding Songs from Egypt* (TR Press, London, 1977).
Translator, with Peter Avery, *The Ruba'iyat of Omar Khayyam* (Allen Lane, London, 1979).
Editor, *Selected Poems of Thomas Gray* (Carcanet, 1981).

DC

POEMS BY JOHN HEATH-STUBBS

The Timeless Nightingale

A nightingale sat perched upon
  The trellis of a Samian vine
Beneath whose shade Anacreon
  Strung his slight lyre, and drank his wine;
Far in the Asian highlands then
  The corpse of great Polycrates
Was scorched by sun and stripped by rain'
  Stretched on the cross-bars of two trees;
But the nightingale's lament
  Was for dismembered Itylus:
White-haired Anacreon vainly schemed –
  How could he move Cleobulus.
    The poet took another glass.

Li Po drank his rice-spirit warm:
  Disgraced at court, he sipped alone –
No-one to talk to or make love –
  Himself, his shadow, and the moon;
Above his head, migrating cranes:
  In the wild gorges monkeys howl:
Red-haired, green-eyed barbarians
  Along the utmost marches prowl;
The nightingale (or what bird else
  Chinese convention had assigned)
Fluted of jewelled gardens where
  Drunken immortals ride the wind.
    The poet took another glass.

Upon a greenish sky at dawn
  The sickle of the moon grew dim:
Hafiz still sat there on the lawn:
  A moon-browed Saki poured for him;
Advanced across the Northern hills
  Timur and his crude Turkish band,
To build their pyramids of skulls,
  And fetch the wine to Samarkand;
But the timeless nightingale
  Enamoured of the eternal rose
Cried "Love's in the dark of the candle-flame,
  And nothing quite what we suppose!"
    The poet took another glass.

The true, the blushful Hippocrene
  Was fairish claret, if you please:
Love a bacillus in his lung,
  John Keats was on those perilous seas;
Into the mills of Yorkshire now
  The Luddite gangs walked stark and grim:
The bourgeois Muse was mousy-haired
  And did not only dance with him;
The nightingale inside his head
  Sang on (at once to him and Ruth)
"You're better off when you are dead –
  Truth's Beauty then, and Beauty truth."
    The poet took another, took another glass.

When Sappho Loved

When Sappho loved a gondolier
Tongues on Lesbos clacked apace:
Unhappily he had no ear
For stanzas of Aeolian grace;
Her lover's leap into the deep
Fishily-tanged Tyrrhenian tide –
One sickening drop – soon put a stop
To lyric passion and to pride.

Lady Mary laughed to view
Great Mr Pope before her kneeling:
His form seemed ill-designed to woo,
Much less evoke an answering feeling:
So Alexander lived to slander
What else he tenderly had sung,
And she confessed among the rest
The Asp of Twickenham's forked tongue.

Dispersed about the Delphic plain
Grasshopper-witted poets thrum –
You, scurrying ants who haul the grain,
Envy them not, though you be dumb:
What's to your mind perhaps you'll find
At harvest's end among the sheaves
But those who follow bright Apollo
Likely embrace cold laurel leaves.

A Cassida for Sadegh Hedayat

(Persian writer, found in a gas-filled room, Paris, 1951)

Like a crested bird from Asia, the East Wind
Has delivered a letter: it says, 'A friend is gone.'

His exile has choked him in an airless chamber:
Sequana, indifferent goddess, mourns in her palaces.

The crested fire-bird, whose nest is increment, hoots
Of oil, education, bank-notes, fanaticism.

But a nightingale lies strangled in the shade of the poplars,
In a spring of irises and unsheathed swords.

Old men with scrolled texts, climbing to towers at evening,
Watch for the new moon, and proclaim a Unity.

In uplands where the morning hunts down fraternal darkness,
And the martyr tulip leaps to a furnace of holy flames.

O routine moon, at the end of fasting, you watch
Inane and beautiful boys inverting their drained glasses.

Sassanid lions lift up their paws in salute;
The clouds are gross that lean down with carbon monoxide.

At Carthage a queen's beauty crumbled to white cinders,
In a prophecy of skies filled with avenging phoenixes.

Those Uranian birds muster from Seoul to Samarkand:
The statue of Apollo weeps on the Palatine.

Virgil's mirror in Mantua is shattered;
The graal of Jamshid is missing; Isaiah is sawn like lumber.

O Rose, can you care if there is one lover the less –
O Rose of Jericho, in a stony region of goats?

He wandered to strange places, like the banished king he was;
He said: 'I am sick of corruption; I shall not come back.'

On airs from India there is a voice that announces:
'The city of mud and pearls has broken another poet.'

To Edmund Blunden

On his 60th Birthday

Thyrsis, or Meliboeus, or old Damoetas –
I must address you
By some such green, Virgilian-vowelled name –
You, the last and truly-tempered voice
Of all our lovely, dead, and pastoral England:
The radio brings that voice to me tonight,
Reading your poem, the vocables
With Kentish loam adhering to them still.
You on the Chinese shore, and I
In Alexandrian garboils? No –
For fourteen years are abrogated now;
The evening sun is gilding Abingdon,
And Kirk White's verse, and Bloomfield's, and Clare's
Our topic as we sit here in the bar,
And brown-haired boys are playing in the street.

Good Night, Ireen

"That which dishonours another man, dishonours me"

I'm Ireen, the Sireen of Soho,
A marginal virgin of culture;
From lunch-time to six in the caf *Chez Alix*
I brood like some gaily-plumed vulture;
From six to eleven in a mild-bitter heaven
I gyrate through waste lands of Fitzravia,
While time's on the wing, like a doll on a string,
With strictly conditioned behaviour.

When shines drunkenly down the full moon on the town
I am spurred into gin-sodden song;
Like some ass-struck Titania with sub-nymphomania,
My heart bares unspeakable wrong;
But more often the charms and the long hairy arms
Of some unwashed companion in exile
For the moment assuage my unquenchable rage –
My emotions, though powerful, are flexile.

My girl-friend, Miss Evelyn Yard
Sophisticate, lesbian, hard,
A flint-breasted Amazon – her pulse beats like hammers on
A heart whence all man's love is barred:
But men, time and again, fall as ruthless as rain
On my starved but hospitable bosom –
Oh infertile delights! Oh Paphian nights!
As I tease them, and please them – to lose 'em!

For I'm Ireen, the Sireen of Soho,
Awaiting the last midnight's tolling,

When all shreds of humanity, gotten in vanity,
    To a Corner-house nook are sent rolling;
When the worm shall explore the ultimate sore
    Which time in my heart has left smouldering,
And a sparse vegetation's the sole indication
    Of the spot in the earth where I'm mouldering.

On the Demolition of the Odeon Cinema, Westbourne Grove

Never one for the flicks, I did not frequent the place:
Though I recall the *Voyage of the Argonauts,*
And a second feature – some twaddle about
A daughter of King Arthur, otherwise unrecorded
By history or tradition. Now, each day,
I pass it, and I hear the brutal noise
Of demolition: clatter of falling masonry,
Machines that seem to grit and grind their teeth,
And munch in gluttony of destruction.

Its soft innards, I guess, are gone already:
The screen, the lighting, the plush seats; the ghosts likewise –
Shadows of shadows, phantoms of phantoms,
The love goddesses, the butcher boy heroes,
The squawking cartoon-animals.

This Odeon – I should regret it? –
In which no ode has ever been recited.
Yet there's a pang – for I've lived long enough
To know that every house of dreams
Must be torn down at last.

Titus and Berenice

"Turn to me in the darkness,
Asia with your cool
Gardens beyond the desert,
Your clear, frog-haunted pool;
I seek your reassurance –
Forget, as I would forget,
Your holy city cast down, the Temple
That still I desecrate."
"Buzz!" said the blue-fly in his head.

"In darkness master me,
Rome with your seven hills,
Roads, rhetorical aqueducts,
And ravaging eagles;
Worlds are at bitter odds, yet we
Can find our love at least –
Not expedient to the Senate,
Abominable to the priest."
"Buzz!" said the blue-fly in his head.

Titus the clement Emperor
And she of Herod's house
Slobbered and clawed each other
Like creatures of the stews;
Lay together, then lay apart
And knew they had not subdued –
She the insect in h8is brain,
Nor he her angry God.

Note: According to a Jewish tradition Titus was afflicted with an insect in his brain as a punishment for his destruction of the Temple.

Letter to David Wright

On his sixtieth birthday

Last year I crossed the meridian of sixty.
Now, David, it's your turn. Old friend, we first met
In your Oxford lodgings, those in the High
With the Churchillian landlady, which afterwards became
A kind of traditional caravanserai
For poets – most of them doomed, of course.
Sidney Keyes' officer's cane
Remained in the hall umbrella stand
Long after his mouth was stopped with Numidian dust.
Allison stayed there on leave, a bird of passage
Migratiing towards his Italian death.
And there was William Bell –
Not war, but a mountain had earmarked him.

Casta Diva

in memory of Maria Callas

Diva – traditional termagant, soprano tantrums,
Scourge of conductors, bane of managers;
Or drifting on a sea of crispéd bank notes
With Plutus in his affluent yacht.

And then retirement – a spectacled, middle-aged lady
Lecturing sensibly on interpretation.

But in the shades the tragic heroines
Mourn for their lost vehicle – La Gioconda,

Tosca, Isolde, murdering Medea;
But most of all I see
A priestess in a Druid grove, who lifts
Clear notes of silver to the silver moon,
Knowing her role of virgin votaress
Is false, who's racked within
With passion, and knowledge of male treachery.

For David Gascoyne

Enter the whirlpool of the fractured images,
Of the deranged senses – descend
Beyond the images into the darkness,
Climbing down its hairy flanks.
In the depth of the darkness, small but persistent,
A glow. It is the sacred hearth.

The voices, the voices – accusing, denouncing,
Mouthing obscenities, nattering and chattering,
They die into the silence: the absolute silence,
Not of the desert, nor the Antarctic waste,
Nor empty spaces between the stars.
In the heart of the silence, the unspoken word,
Its name is Love – the Christ
Of revolution and of poetry.

Pearse Hutchinson

(b. 1927)

ABOUT THE POET Pearse Hutchinson (b.1927)

Pearse Hutchinson was born in an Irish family in Glasgow in 1927. His father Harry Hutchinson, a printer, was also the Sinn Féin's treasurer in Glasgow and was interned in Frognoch in 1919-21. His mother Cathleen Sara wanted to raise their son in 'holy Catholic Ireland' and Eamon de Valera found a job for Harry Hutchinson in Dublin. So Pearse grew up in the Irish capital and studied at University College Dublin. He currently resides in Dublin.

A polyglot, he worked as a translator in Geneva in the early 1950s and then lived in Spain for almost a decade. A distinguished literary translator from Irish, Catalan, Flemish, Galician, French and Italian, he has published a series of translations from Italian, Catalan and Galaico-Portuguese. In recent years his own poetry has been translated into Castilian, Italian and Galician. Hutchinson has also worked as a teacher and broadcaster. Jointly with Eileann Ní Chuilleanain, he is the founder-editor of *Cyphers*.

Pearse Hutchinson writes poetry in both Irish and English. Many consider him a champion of Gaelic writing: "To kill a language is to kill one's self", he has written in one of his poems. His lyrical and compassionate poems have established him as one of modern Ireland's finest poets. His *Collected Poems* was published on his 75th birthday. His numerous awards include the Butler Prize for Gaelic Writing (1969) and an Irish Arts Council bursary (1978). The University of Leeds appointed him as Gregory Fellow in Poetry from 1971 to 1973. A member of the elite body for the arts in Ireland, Aosdána, he lives in Dublin. The artist Edward Maguire has drawn his portrait.

SELECT BIBLIOGRAPHY

POETRY COLLECTIONS

Tongue Without Hands (Dolmen Press, Dublin, 1963).
Faoistin Bhacach (Báile Átha Cliath, An Clórhomhar, 1968).
Expansions (Dolmen Press, 1969).
Watching the Morning Grow (Gallery Press, Dublin, 1972).
The Frost is All Over (Gallery Press, 1975).
Selected Poems (Gallery Press, 1982).
Climbing the Light (Gallery Press, 1985).
The Soul that Kissed the Body (Gallery Press, 1991).
Barnsley Main Seam (Gallery Press, 1995).
Collected Poems (Gallery Press, 2002).

POETRY TRANSLATIONS

Joseph Carner, 30 Poems (Dolphin Books, Oxford, 1970).
Done into English (Gallery Press, Oldcastle, 2002).

DC

POEMS BY PEARSE HUTCHINSON

Málaga

for Sammy Sheridan

The scent of unseen jasmine on the warm night beach.

The tram along the sea road all the way from town
through its wide open sides drank unseen jasmine down.
Living was nothing all those nights but that strong flower,
whose hidden voice on darkness grew to such mad power
I could have sworn for once I travelled through full peace
and even love at last had perfect calm release
only by breathing in the unseen jasmine scent,
that ruled us and the summer every hour we went.

The tranquil unrushed wine drunk on the daytime beach.
Or from an open room all that our sight could reach
was heat, sea, light, unending images of peace;
and then at last the night brought jasmine's great release –
not images but calm uncovetous content,
the wide-eyed heart alert at rest in June's own scent.

In daytime's humdrum town from small child after child
we bought cluster on cluster of the star flower's wild
white widowed heads, re-wired on strong weed stalks they'd trimmed
to long green elegance; but still the whole month brimmed
at night along the beach with a strong voice like peace;
and each morning the mind stayed crisp in such release.

Some hint of certainty, still worth longing I could teach,
lies lost in a strength of jasmine down a summer beach.

Gaeltacht

Bartley Costello, eighty years old
sat in his silver-grey tweeds on a kitchen chair,
at his door in Carraroe, the sea only yards away,
smoking a pipe, with a pint of porter beside his boot:
Tor the past twenty years I've eaten nothing only
periwinkles, my own hands got them off those rocks.
You're a quarter my age, if you'd stick to them winkles
you'd live as long as me, and keep as spry.'
In the Liverpool Bar, at the North Wall,
on his way to join his children over there,
an old man looked at me, then down at his pint
of rich Dublin stout. He pointed at the black glass:
'Is lu i an Ghaeilge na an t-uisce sa ngloine sin.'
Beartia Confhaola, prime of his manhood,
driving between the redweed and the rock-fields,
driving through the sunny treeless quartz glory ofCarna,
answered the foreigner's glib pity, pointing at the
small black cows: 'You won't get finer anywhere
than those black porry cattle.' In a pub near there,
one of the locals finally spoke to the townie:
'Labhraim Ie strainsein. Creidim gur choir bheith
ag labhairt Ie strainsein.' Proud as a man who'd claim:
'I made an orchard of a rock-field,
bougainvillea clamber my turf-ricks.'
A Dublin tourist on a red-quarter strand
hunting firewood found the ruins of a boat,
started breaking the struts out- an old man came,
he shook his head, and said:
'Aa, a mhac: na bi ag briseadh baid.'
The low walls of rock-fields in the west

are a beautiful clean white. There are chinks between
the neat white stones to let the wind through safe,
you can see the blue sun through them.
the walls grow higher, get grey:
an ugly grey. And the chinks disappear:
through those walls you can see nothing.
Then at last you come to the city,
beautiful with salmon basking becalmed black below
a bridge over the pale-green Corrib; and ugly
with many shopkeepers looking down on men like
Bartley Costello and Beartla Confhaola because they
speak in Irish, eat periwinkles, keep
small black porry cattle, and on us
because we are strangers.

Wouldn't I?

When I'm in your arms, do I think about death?
When I'm in your lovely young arms
I'm far too busy enjoying
being in your arms.
When I'm not in your arms or your company,
that fearful, despicable maniac still
crosses my mind now and then but
almost never stops me in my tracks
bleakly staring as far too often and long
in the ageing decade before
you took me by summer storm.
Let the stern shake their heads, I shan't
get my comeuppance any worse than them;
I never did think much of all

that Eros-Thanatos-inextricable
wisdom of ages. Hubris
has nowt to do with it, it's just
that love's about life not death,
I'm scarcely afraid any more -
tho' when it comes to the point and at my
age it could happen any minute - but in
the meantime and
three years next month is not too bad
as meantimes go though here I am
trying to thank you for this in particular and so
for the space of a poem ipso facto mentioning
the bully more often than usual, I wouldn't
go so far as to claim
you've made the wretch irrelevant
but it doesn't seem to matter so much any more,
love can
                    work wonders.

A True Story Ending in False Hope

for Martin Collins

The barman vaulted the counter
landing with a fine clutter
beside our musical table;
he nearly upsets the pints
of all the dominical couples.
'We'll have no music here,'
he roared, bursting a blood-vessel.
We weren't, in fact, a steel-band,
or a demolition-squad,

so Justin gestured the tin-whistle
towards the married couples:
'Does anyone mind this
                                        music?'
Some said they didn't,
the rest sang dumb,
but one old woman spoke up loudly:
'We like it,' she cried,
'it brightens things up a bit here.'
The barman burst another vessel.
'Out! Out!' he shouted.
'We'll finish our drink,' said the Corkman,
the Corkman who'd *asked* for the music,
and we did,
but we left –
uttering suitable imprecations.

We crossed the unmusical road,
skirting a public jax
that hadn't yet turned into a ghost,
boarded a chopper for heaven,
and played and drank till closing-time,
thinking how musical
Ireland
        will
            be.

Look, No Hands

for Ernie Hughes

Lengua sin manos, cuemo osas fablar?
- Poema del Cid

I blame old women for buying paper roses,
yet pluck a dandelion: by the time
it reaches my lapel it's turned to paper.

I hate the winter, and blame drinkers
for hiding in dark pubs when the sun shines outside,
and could be enjoyed at sidewalk tables;
yet every time I visit a crowded beach
I bring a sun-ray lamp along.

I praise trust above all,
yet cannot let a friend post a letter
in case he might stop on the way for a drink.

I admire a stone for its hardness,
resembling it only in barrenness;
admire a butterfly's brightness
resembling it only in brittleness.

I like speed, summer, the country roads,
but never could master a bike.
Believing in God because of the need to praise –
though fear alone, so far, makes me long to pray –
if granted another hundred years
I might learn
how to say prayers.

Amhrán na mBréag*

after the Irish of Micheál Mharcais Ó Conghaile

In the middle of the wood I set sail
as the bee and the bat were at anchor just off shore
I found in the sea's rough shallows a nest of bees
In a field's ear I saw
a mackerel milking a cow
I saw a young woman in Greece boiling the city of Cork over the kitchen fire
Last night, in a serpent's ear, I slept sound
I saw an eel with a whip in her hand whipping a shark ashore
MacDara's Island told me he never saw more wonders:
a kitten washing a salmon in the river
the music-mast of a ship being
conceived in a cat's arse
a badger in the nest of an eagle milking a cow
and a sparrow wielding a hammer putting a keel on a boat.

* The Song of Lies

The Miracle of Bread and Fiddles

We were so hungry
we turned bark into bread.

But still we were hungry,
so we turned clogs into fiddles.

James Kirkup

(b. 1923)

MY JAMES KIRKUP

Thirty-odd years after it is difficult to be precise about dates. It may have been in 1959, when I was a sixth-former at an horrendously repressive Leeds grammar school, or the year following when I was teaching 'unqualified' at an inner city primary school, or perhaps the year after that, when I was a student at Leeds Teachers' Training College but somewhere in that period I came across the poetry of James Kirkup.

It was about the time I was starting to write poetry myself and of living poets Kirkup was rapidly to become my master, mentor and model. Why Kirkup? Perhaps most of all because he mirrored my own sense of alienation, that special alienation all true poets feel when they realise that their vocation, instead of drawing them closer to their fellow-men as they might wish, makes them stand alone:

And he must go
The lonelier for his unwanted miracle,
His singular way, a gentle lunatic at large
In the societies of cross and reasonable men
('The Poet')

As well as his poetry Kirkup wrote two excellent autobiographies of childhood, *The Only Child* and *Sorrows, Passions and Alarms* which chart the poignant years of his growing up on Tyneside in the period just after the end of the first World War. Recently I re-read them and found their magic still worked. With great skill Kirkup portrays the life of the poet-to-be from birth to early adulthood. Scenes from working-class life – bath-night and working-day are caught in delightful detail with rainbow suds, mangle and all. A working class background is a powerful preparation for a life devoted to poetry, provided it is not too 'deprived'. Certainly the working class life I enjoyed in Leeds in the forties was quite wonderful. It wasn't, of course, a life of council estates, drug-gangs and ghetto-blasters. It was a life of *community*, shared values and – in hard times – shared food. Above all it was having a sense of being cared for and protected, not just by one's parents but by neighbours and by other children. I try to capture this in my poem 'The Bridge Over the Aire':

But no child in the streets
Ever fought another,
We were all everyone's
Sister or brother
Whenever anyone fell
There was always someone
Near to kiss you better

(from 'Against the Grain', stanza 34,
Book I of *The Bridge Over the Aire*)

It's sad that Kirkup himself never wrote poetry about his childhood. What we have in his work is a glimpse into the poet's inner world, arcane and fascinating, where figures move in an underwater dream-ballet:

there where at evening a misted lake is laid away
like a remembered silence in an angry day

('Homage to Vaslav Nijinsky')

Prefacing the first volume of the *Collected Works* of Paul Éluard, Lucien Scheler wrote, 'Il y a une magie créatrice chez Éluard toute personelle' and so it is with Kirkup also.

The ambience of his work is music, painting, ballet, the theatre and nineteenth century French poetry, but it is also a poetry of life, as well as art:

These are the children bred by war, whose lives
fret at their ignorance of peace.
There is no answer to the question they have raised no hand to ask.

('In a London Schoolroom')

When I first read Kirkup's poems I had moved to Yeadon, a mill-village between Leeds and Bradford. I yearned to be a poet and Kirkup seemed unquestionably that, totally and unambiguously. His poetry rippled with the music of the soul:

O, the dark note of the thrummed guitar,
electric strings parallel with thrilling fingers,
haunted mouth drugged with the sorrows of a hidden sun

('Negro Spirituals')

I would sit on the bus to Leeds with a book of Kirkup's poems to enliven the journey, hoping that one day I might have a book of my own in print! I wrote to Kirkup, care of the PEN Club in London and some weeks later to my great amazement and joy received a reply on scented *washi*!

By this time I had left training college and I was teaching a class of wonderfully-gifted ten-year olds. Kirkup's letter arrived on my first morning at the school, so it must have been in September1964:

I stood there in front of forty-five faces
The first day of term, not especially fancying
'Exercises in Mechanical Arithmetic' and so instead
I read a poem from Kirkup in Japan, about Nijinsky
Hand-written on a fan of washi.

('Wyther Park School Leeds Five')

The sixties was a great time for poetry in Leeds, so much so that an American academic is writing a book called 'The Leeds Poetry Renaissance'. As one commentator put it, 'Poetry was falling from the air'. Kirkup was the first Gregory Fellow in Poetry at Leeds University, but this was while I was still at school. During his stay in the city he wrote 'Wreath Makers: Leeds Market', one of his best-known poems:

A cocksure boy in the gloom of the gilded market bends
With blunt fingers a bow of death and the flowers work with him
They fashion a grave of grass with dead bracken and fine ferns.

And here a grieving flower god with a lyre in his arms
Tumbles mute strings in the rough-gentle machine of his fingers
His eyes wet violets, and in his mouth a last carnation.

Anyone who knows Leeds Kirkgate Market will not be surprised that its magical atmosphere sparked off such a lyrical response. Harold Gilman did a beautiful painting of the market which hangs in the Tate. It gets a passing mention in a poem of Tony Harrison's and I managed a simultaneous homage to both Kirkup and Kirkgate:

James Kirkup, I think of you,
Exiled in Japan, your poem,

'Wreath Makers, Leeds, Market,'
Making me a poet.

('A Sad Heart in Leeds Market')

From Kirkup I learnt to look around my own city:

Dear, you and I, the prisoners within this hard and heavy place
Must sweeten our captivity with these small signs of grace;
Like masters of a special craft, a dying art,
Attempt to make the best of the materials at hand,
Yet always longing for the wines, the lighter heart,

The music and the fountains of a gentler land.
(James Kirkup: 'Summertime in Leeds')

Kirkup's only novel, *The Love of Others* (1962) is a minor masterpiece and deserves to be recognised as such. It is as much a prose poem as a novel in which psychological penetration is matched with erotic fantasy of the highest order.

For years Jamie and I exchanged letters and poems. During this period he published best-selling travel books and a whole series of translations from a bewildering variety of languages, including Polish. These translations were works of art in themselves and many of them I read aloud to my class of ten year olds in those wonderful far-off days. He also wrote plays and his version of Dürrenmatt's *The Physicist* – specially commissioned by Peter Brook for the Royal Shakespeare Company – was televised in 1964.

No one in the literary world gave me the consistent support and encouragement I had from James Kirkup over a number of years. It is very sad that eventually I had to sell all his beautiful letters to me in order to survive. Perhaps they will turn up in a university library and one day I shall be able to reread them!

Perhaps Kirkup's most important poem from this period is 'The Child, the Woman and the Man'. It is not an easy poem to quote from as every line is integral to its layered structure. It begins with 'the child':

his head
Wild with the message of the winter sea,
In his head a magic stone

Then it moves on to 'the woman':

He is the agony she knows
When she must deliver herself
Of life, yet go on living.

And finally, 'the Man':

He is the one who acts upon the rock
That is himself and with an angel's hand
Draws forth the water we must drink
For our survival in the desert

From 1970 to 1995 I wrote no poetry and my reading was largely in the field of psychoanalysis. When my inspiration returned and I began to look around the literary world I was shocked to see how Kirkup's work had been marginalised. With the honourable exception of William Oxley (*Completing the Picture*) anthologists* simply omitted Kirkup. Yet his work is so wonderfully accessible to readers of all ages and temperaments:

You must not mind, old girl, as shame comes hunting you:
Try to preserve, as I do, this unruffled air ...
Yes, dear, this is hell, and this is me confronting you
('To an Old Lady Asleep at a Poetry Reading')

When I was in my last year as a student at Leeds Teachers' Training College I was allowed to submit a folio of my own poems as part of my final examinations. I was given a *viva* by Professor Valentine Cunningham of Leicester University, the college's external examiner, and I was delighted to discover he had actually met Jamie and shared my enthusiasm for his work!

Once Jamie was planning to visit London and he suggested we meet 'under the statue of Eros in Piccadilly Circus' but he cancelled at the last minute and I felt a sense of relief – the picture I had built up of him was so idealised that no human being could possibly live up to it!

Many years ago I wrote an article for *Peace News* entitled 'James Kirkup: the Forgotten Poet' and I began with a quotation from Jamie's first letter to me:

Most of all I am touched by your admiration for the true qualities of my poetry, qualities which most people seem unwilling or unable to recognise... But I have been so wounded by deliberate refusal to recognise the sort of thing I say and the way I say it that I feel incapacitated for the rest of my days.

I went on to castigate the literary establishment of the day (circa 1965) for their lack of interest in Kirkup's work. At least he was included in Kenneth Allott's *Penguin Book of Contemporary Verse*, but his introductory comment was most unjust:

Mr Kirkup has a lively eye and an enviable facility. He is at his best as a versatile poetic reporter absorbed in some scene or incident which he brings alive on paper with rapid verbal strokes, weakest when he is directly concerned with his own private feelings.

Allott is simply wrong about Kirkup's gifts – 'Fading Grass' is one of the most moving poems I've read on the subject of loss and loneliness:

The sun's candour and the sky's deep light;
The river that by day
Is shallow and profound at night
Give no comfort, for all sight
Is empty now you are away.

Time only makes me feel how life must go
In nothingness without
The time you give me for the love I owe:
How longing lasts beyond the griefs we know
How all things die and suns go out.

Essentially it is as a lyric poet that Kirkup moves and inspires us and so his poetry is, like all lyrical poetry, as Cyril Connolly pointed out, ultimately unanalysable:

There is a new world, and a new man
Who walks amazed that he so long

Was blind and dumb, he who runs
towards the sun

Lifts up a trustful face in skilful song
And fears no more the darkness where
his day began.

This is a stanza from 'There is a New Morning' and if this isn't good poetry then I don't know what is. Yet only one critic, Robin Skelton in *The Poetic Pattern*, has given it the attention it deserves.

The French psychoanalyst André Green has written about the paradox of 'absence of presence' and 'presence of absence' but it is the poet James Kirkup who has so movingly actualised the paradox:

The lights go on, casting their nets across the lawn
In a bright box you move, your hair is golden-brown.
Above a chimney-pot the first star like a spark is blown.

Now I will go along the cliffs and by the silent farm,
Across the fields already cold. But turn
To look toward you, often, till the blinds are drawn.
('The Parting')

I was delighted when Salzburg University re-printed James Kirkup's poetry and so made it once again available to a wide audience. I felt honoured when I was asked to contribute to this *festschrift*. Nothing matters more to a poet than *to be encouraged.* When I needed help and support Kirkup was always there, year in, year out. That is how I remember him; that is why I honour him.

*Kirkup has, of course, been published in many school and student anthologies at home and abroad, but seldom in mainstream anthologies.

BT

ABOUT THE POET James Kirkup (b. 1918)

James Falconer Kirkup was born in Sunderland on April 23, 1918. He was educated at South Shields High School and Durham University.

His poems regularly appeared in *The Listener* from 1949 to 1965 and a number were broadcast on BBC radio. From 1950 to 1952 he was appointed as Gregory Fellow in Poetry at the University of Leeds, and the university's library houses a special collection of his literary papers. Kirkup's autobiographical *The Only Child* (1957) is a memorable account of a working-class northern childhood.

From the 1960s he held academic posts in Japan, including a Professorship in English Literature at Kyoto University from 1977, and published many books on Japan, including *Japan Marine* (1965) and *Paper Windows: Poems from Japan* (1968). He was Literary Editor of *Orient/West Magazine* in Tokyo and in 1966 he founded *Poetry Nippon* in Nagoya. Japanese forms of poetry, particularly the haiku, greatly influenced his work.

In 1977 his homoerotic poem about Christ, published in *Gay News*, gave rise to the first prosecution for over fifty years under Britain's blasphemy libel law. Denis Lemon, the editor, was fined and given a suspended sentence. But the banned poem was widely distributed at demonstrations and is readily available on the internet. Though far from being his best work, 'The Love that Dares to Speak its Name' (its title inspired by the poem 'Two Loves' by Oscar Wilde's companion Alfred Douglas) is Kirkup's best-known poem. Mortified by the extreme response to his poem, both by those like Mary Whitehouse who attacked it and by those who supported it, Kirkup chose to leave Britain in the same year and still lives in Andorra. "I disapprove of all politics and all politicians," he has said.

A Fellow of the Royal Society of Literature, Kirkup is a novelist, translator, playwright and travel writer. He is also perhaps one of the most prolific poets of the 20th century, and is still publishing. His volumes of poetry include *A Correct Compassion* (1952), *The Descent into the Cave* (1957), *Paper Windows* (1968), and *A Bewick Bestiary* (1971). In 1996 the University of Salzburg published much of his poetry from Japan in three volumes.

Kirkup's many honours include the Atlantic-Rockefeller Award in 1950, the Japan P.E.N. Club International literary prize in 1965, the Batchelder Award for translation in 1968, the Keats Prize in 1974 and the Scott-Moncrieff prize for translation in 1993.

SELECT BIBLIOGRAPHY

POETRY COLLECTIONS

A Correct Compassion and Other Poems (Oxford University Press, London, 1952).

The Descent into the Cave and Other Poems (Oxford University Press, 1957).

The Prodigal Son (Oxford University Press, 1959).

Paper Windows:Poems from Japan (Dent, London, 1968).

White Shadows, Black Shadows: Poems of Peace and War (Dent, 1970).

A Bewick Bestiary (Northumberland Arts Group, 1971).

The Body Servant: Poems of Exile (Dent, 1971).

Throwback: Poems Towards an Autobiography (Rockingham Press, Ware, 1992).

Look at it This Way:Poems for Young People (Rockingham Press, 1992).

Omens of Disaster: Selected Shorter Poems, vol. 1 (University of Salzburg, 1996).

Once and For All: Selected Shorter Poems, vol. 2 (University of Salzburg, 1996).

An Extended Breath: Collected Longer Poems and Sequences (University of Salzburg, 1996).

OTHER

The Only Child: An Autobiography of Infancy (Collins, London, 1957).
The Love of Others (Collins, 1962)
An Actor's Revenge: A Kabuki Opera (Faber Music, London, 1989).
Insect Summer (Knopf, New York, 1971).
The Magic Drum (Knopf, 1973).
I, of All People (Weidenfeld and Nicholson, London, 1990).
Gaizin on the Ginja (Peter Owen, London, 1992).
A Poet Could Not But be Gay (Peter Owen, 1992).
Queens Have Died Young and Fair (Peter Owen, 1994).

DC

POEMS BY JAMES KIRKUP

The Love That Dares to Speak its Name

As they took him from the cross
I, the centurion, took him in my arms –
the tough lean body
of a man no longer young,
beardless, breathless,
but well hung.

He was still warm.
While they prepared the tomb
I kept guard over him.
His mother and the Magdalen
had gone to fetch clean linen
to shroud his nakedness.

I was alone with him.
For the last time
I kissed his mouth. My tongue
found his, bitter with death.
I licked his wound –
the blood was harsh

For the last time
I laid my lips around the tip
of that great cock, the instrument
of our salvation, our eternal joy.
The shaft, still throbbed, anointed
with death's final ejaculation.

I knew he'd had it off with other men –
with Herod's guards, with Pontius Pilate,
With John the Baptist, with Paul of Tarsus
with foxy Judas, a great kisser, with
the rest of the Twelve, together and apart.
He loved all men, body, soul and spirit. – even me.

So now I took off my uniform, and, naked,
lay together with him in his desolation,
caressing every shadow of his cooling flesh,
hugging him and trying to warm him back to life.
Slowly the fire in his thighs went out,
while I grew hotter with unearthly love.

It was the only way I knew to speak our love's proud name,
to tell him of my long devotion, my desire, my dread –
something we had never talked about. My spear, wet with blood,
his dear, broken body all open wounds,
and in each wound his side, his back,
his mouth – I came and came and came

as if each coming was my last.
And then the miracle possessed us.
I felt him enter into me, and fiercely spend
his spirit's final seed within my hole, my soul,
pulse upon pulse, unto the ends of the earth –
he crucified me with him into kingdom come.

– This is the passionate and blissful crucifixion
same-sex lovers suffer, patiently and gladly.
They inflict these loving injuries of joy and grace
one upon the other, till they die of lust and pain

within the horny paradise of one another's limbs,
with one voice cry to heaven in a last divine release.

Then lie long together, peacefully entwined, with hope
of resurrection, as we did, on that green hill far away.
But before we rose again, they came and took him from me.
They knew no what we had done, but felt
no shame or anger. Rather they were glad for us,
and blessed us, as would he, who loved all men.

And after three long, lonely days, like years,
in which I roamed the gardens of my grief
seeking for him, my one friend who had gone from me,
he rose from sleep, at dawn, and showed himself to me before
all others. And took me to him with

the love that now forever dares to speak its name.

Emily in Winter

Born in December, from the start
you knew a sunstruck winter of the heart.

Gales now blow clouds of snowdust ghosts, that bloom
with rainbows round your black-railed room.

I come once more with flowers and alone
to speak with you behind your stone.

You who can move upon the crusted whitenesses
and leave no track; I press

my handprint on the snow, and feel the heat
above the buried breastbone where your heart once beat.

Summertime in Leeds

Yes, the cruel city has relaxed, and wears
A flushed, unbuttoned look. Beneath a shrewd
Provincial mask the citizen displays
Some traces of bucolic heat, a rural vacancy.
The rustic ancestry now frequently appears
In ladies moving dreamily as cattle through the streets
And larger stores, where, with their great friends
The treat themselves, the hoydens of the fashionable set,
To cakes, tea, talk, and the suburban scandal of a cigarette.

A smart hat cannot quite conceal the grimy
Shepherdess; the backside of an honest fishwife is politely glossed
Beneath the crumpled chic of fashions for the fuller
Figure: and the nice crisp blouse
Beneath plump arms betrays the decent sweat
Of milkmaids in the well-groomed undergraduette.
Keen on cricket, the chaps from the office are out for a sporting stroll,
        and girls
Are perched like haycocks on the public lawns, where swains in
        Business suitings lie,
Digesting hot, expensive, colourless and tasteless shepherd's pie.

So, too, in the most unexpected places, the severe
And sombre city wears a brave and country air.

In back streets, blades of green pierce through the stones.
A hawthorn on a siding, that was once
A wildflower lane, seems to be fizzing with original leaves,
And in the solemn parks, somewhere behind the floral ranks,
The holly, black as iron, blazes with shoots of primal innocence.
– Dear, you and I, the prisoners within this hard and heavy place,
Must sweeten our captivity with these small signs of grace;

Like masters of a special craft, a dying art,
Attempt to make the best of the material at hand,
Yet always longing for the wines, the lighter heart,
The music and the fountains of a gentler land.

In a London Schoolroom

Arms in cool dresses shine, boys' throats are bare,
the murmuring blackboards quiver in a haze of chalk.
Summer has come, but will not enter
these open windows that the sunlight
blinds with heat and shutters with despair.
The tree of hands and faces tosses in the gales of talk.
A flashing desk-lid like a bomb explodes,
spelling disaster, the final tree of dust.

These are the children bred by war, whose lives
fret at their ignorance of peace. There is no answer
to the question they have raised no hand to ask,
no cloudless holiday that would release
life that is sick, hope that was never there,
no task make plain the words they cannot learn to trust.
Not we, who fail to understand, but only time can teach
a lesson they will not forget, and educate with pain
these last pretenders of an innocence they know is vain.

To an Old Lady Asleep at a Poetry Reading

(Of Dame Edith Sitwell's 'Still Falls the Rain')

Snore on in your front-row chair! Let not my voice
Disturb the wordless heaven that your eyes have found!
I, too, would welcome that release,
Here in this hard hall with the naked lights
In which my spirit and my words are bound,
The nightmare setting of all sleepless nights.

Why do the others, too, not briefly dose?
My voice has laid a healthy spell
Upon your gentle fret, and on a mind that glows
Still with a small but vivid fire.
They surely feel the moderate enchantment just as well?
Why do we all not sleep, abandoning these platforms that do more
than tire?

Dear Lady, do not let that wakeful vulture,
Your tiresome neighbour, provoke you with her nudging gloom.
She is one of those restless seekers after culture,
Guardians of Beauty who at Question-time will always shout for it;
While I desire only the chilly sanctuary of the chairman's guestroom.
Let her be in on everything: you're better out of it!

Poor dear, she's wakened you. The sweet sleep sours.
Snug in your old fur-coat, you stare
Perplexed a moment, from under your hat's provincial flowers.
– You must not mind, old girl, as shame comes hunting you:
Try to preserve, as I do, this unruffled air …
Yes, dear, this is hell, and this is me confronting you.

The Poet

Each instant of his life a task, he never rests,
And works most when he appears to be doing nothing.
The least of it is putting down in words
What usually remains unwritten and unspoken,
And would so often be much better left
Unsaid, for it is really the unspeakable
That he must try to give an ordinary tongue to.

And if, by art and accident,
He utters the unutterable, then
It must appear as natural as breath,
Yet be an inspiration. And he must go,
The lonelier for his unwanted miracle,
His singular way, a gentle lunatic at large
In the societies of cross and reasonable men.

Paul Mills

(b. 1948)

ABOUT THE POET Paul Mills (b. 1948)

Paul Mills was born in 1948, the youngest of the dozen Gregory Fellows whose poetry is presented in this anthology. The University of Leeds appointed him as Gregory Fellow in Poetry from 1976 to 1978. The university's Brotherton Library has collected some of his papers.

During the 1980s Mills and his family moved to California where he lectured in English Literature and travelled round the western United States. But he returned to England, became a single parent and a Lecturer in the School of Literature at the College of Ripon and York St John at York.

He has had three poetry collections published by Carcanet. In the autobiographical *Half Moon Bay* he explores the issues concerning parenthood, marriage, gender, nationhood and independence. A fourth collection, *Dinosaur Point*, was published by Smith/Doorstop Books when he won the Poetry Business Competition in 1999.

Two of Mills' plays have been performed at the Royal National Theatre and at the West Yorkshire Playhouse. His book on creative writing, *Writing in Action*, published by Routledge, has been a successful textbook for creative writers.

Ted Hughes has said of Mills' poetry: "What I especially like is the rather apprehensive feeling that absolutely anything can happen … a big kit of metaphysical templates."

SELECT BIBLIOGRAPHY

POETRY COLLECTIONS

Trio: New Poets from Edinburgh – Roderick Watson, Valeries Simmons, Paul Mills (New Rivers, New York, 1971).
North Carriageway (Carcanet, Manchester, 1976).

Third Person (Carcanet, 1978).
Half Moon Bay (Carcanet, 1993).
Dinosaur Point (Smith/Doorstop, Huddersfield, 1999).

OTHER

Writing in Action (Routledge, London, 1996).

DC

POEMS BY PAUL MILLS

Brenda

'Who's Brenda?' my bank-manager is asking,
his eyes on the item of £40 a week,
seeing some lavish fantasy on the side
eating the family budget.
When I give him the picture
he smiles – 'Cut it.'

In spite of the sink, slime on the washed-up
cutlery, we were thriving.
Yet you insisted we get some woman in,
some reliable substitute for you.
We interviewed one person and employed her,
matron in humour and girth, slightly insane,
a prison visitor who had married a murderer.
We found this exotic but she couldn't cook.

And you with her wasn't much of a fit,
she with her inbred British fear of the young,
their awful permissive speech and eating habits,
her policeman-father bringing up kids strictly,
not like ours – echoing neighbours' complaints.
And what they were saying about them all over town,
waiting by the school gates. She took you aside,
passed it all on. 'What they need is discipline.
He's hopeless.' In other words – Their Mother.

You believed it.
How could you not believe it?

All that expense just so you could hear it –
'Fathers can't cope. Especially *him*.
The children need you. You!'

Music to you.

And this was your only fault in this story,
allowing this woman to tell you your business,
this woman to whom, otherwise,
you would never have given the time of day.
I didn't need the bank manager's advice.

I knew the point against her was being proved,
that her white-haired motherly British judgements
would be taken down and not put back,
that our life was seeing the end of Brenda.
But two hundred and forty-five miles apart,
your problem wasn't solved – how to be a mother
and not a mother – how to make these ends meet.

The Common Talk

Who do they see by the sink when they come home?
Against whose rules ditching skateboards,
bags of books, kit, junk in the hall?
No clay pot in the garden without fag-end.
Never any corner without its sock.
Telling the time by what's gone off in the fridge.
Walking the timeless aisles of supermarkets.
Writing sick-notes, seeing washing done.
Inventing rules for dishes, dope – No Dope,

stay-over guests and length of stay of guests,
yes then no then yes, and use of the car, the phone,
money, standing unmarked in constant request-field,
waking up to the youth of the town breathing
in every room, the house chirping. Who in his right mind?

News From Nowhere

Columns crack with gossip. Charles, Diana.
Pictures of her with handsome riding instructor.
Pictures of him solemnly smiling it off,
as if they were a couple just like us,
he on the far side of thirty, two nice kids.

So we think how lucky to be us and happy.
We are the way it should be. They are not.
Our kitchen isn't like their kitchen.
What's this on the cover of the New York Star?
Who's who in the latest Who's Who
of fucking? Rage. Impotent
forefingered gesture at her supposed calm.
Cost to the crown etc becoming mesmeric
in his eyes only and down his shirt-front possibly
in dribbles. Leaks out of the bed into the press.

Poor Charles. Poorer Diana. What's happened
to this marriage of innocents now that America
has its teeth in the sheets, is ripping them up,
searching for stains, truculence, depression?
Aren't we pleased we have a Republic,
Equality. Entertain friends. Innocence. Love each other.

A Balinese Mask

You gave me this for my American birthday.
Carved wood painted dazzling white.
Chin, teeth, lips, cheekbones stretched
into a permanent face-altering smile.

That was the end of March, and for yours,
four days later, I bought you a poster,
the image of an art deco hotel – Miami Beach –
a blonde with a man walking towards a convertible.
Man, woman, hotel-front, shades and car
Movie style in silkscreen monocolour.

Obviously we both had a taste for shape,
simplicity, yet your present to me
was the more powerful.
Instead of something flickering in one corner,
this smile carved its whole face. It was ecstatic.
Wouldn't release either of us one bit
from the noise and stretch of it.

It's years now since you retrieved your present,
while this mask still hangs here in my house.
A souvenir – but of what? Part of a life?
How much has been carved out by this smile?
This permanent pain-shaped shout of joy?

I don't know what it was to the people of Bali,
worn for what carnival or ceremony,
so clearly a smile – angled another way
a suffering face. Yet when I look

at our daughter now, at our son,
under my skin the smile feels its way back.

Single Parent

Hearing what my colleagues worry about,
being who I am is so much easier.
No one talks of closing this family down.
No one talks , or not in our house,
about quality, curriculum solvency,
skill-oriented aims, learning outcomes,
recruitment drives, value for money,
not even occasionally 'sabbaticals'.

There aren't any. And the managers – us –
don't deliberately fail to minute items,
don't minute any items at all,
don't decide on items of major consequence
nobody gets to know about till later,
don't publish the outcome of their discussions
in some office-speak of ultimate secrecy,
don't even meet, except for one or two talks
each month on the phone.

'Your tea's in the oven, wash everything up,
cuddle the cat, (feed it first),
don't make a noise if you're late
and I'm asleep when you come in,
and switch off lights – love M' works ok here.
Sorting the gist's easier than running a faculty.

So give me a house where meetings
are in constant consultation,
constant ferment, all intellectual wars
wholly admitted, where the slop bucket's
not dressed up as 'interim appraisal',
'mission statement', 'adopting
positive strategies towards change',
or the menu's twelve months in advance.

Nor do we have a problem about recruitment.
Under every bed there's another bed.
Under that another. We are equipped.
I think work could learn a lot from home –
trying to get things done by the surest means,
which is that the reason too must please,
listening to them, learning that if things
go wrong it's probably my fault.

Christmas Day

Not far from the age your mother was
the year I met her – summer of '77,
you're in a Castro café called 'The Café'
December '99 – writing your diary,
e-mailing chunks home –
'Random people stop and chat to us
wearing such bright colours.
You wouldn't find English families
walking around in the same T-shirt and caps.
It's bizarre. I feel like a piece of driftwood,
as in the Travis song. This time I'm here

no longer in the wake of my parents.
I've broken off from the tree
and am just floating. It feels good.'
Then from Santa Barbara a week later –
'It's like discovering new, rare breeds.
Richard, the witty, black dude
who smokes weed through a pipe.
The oldish French woman I suddenly
started dancing with at breakfast.
The woman in shades and a scarf who walked around
like she was some kind of celebrity in hiding.
Danny the old guy who cooks and drinks much vodka.
John the good-looking guy with painful stubble.'
And then later –
'Venice Beach on a Sunday is just like Golden Gate Park
but there are far and many more mad people per square metre.
And you can get a beach massage for only $5.
I hope I don't feel family-sick (note that it won't be
homesick, England is miserable) on Christmas Day.'
What shall I say? Some words really do it,
and you've found them. These are yours,
next to mine and worlds away
from puddles, streets, December, work,
yet who could be more pleased to hear them,
feel them shine across our dark.
Easy as speech they crash out with you,
wake when you wake,
colouring your country of the sun.

Peter Redgrove

(1932 – 2003)

PETER REDGROVE

While a student at Leeds Training College, I supplemented my course by attending classes at Leeds University run by the then Gregory Fellow in Poetry, Jon Silkin, followed by the sour, dour Scots poet Bill Price Turner and finally Peter Redgrove. I shall never forget the evening I went, with great difficulty, to Guiseley Town Hall to hear him give a reading. The hall was packed and Redgrove had already begun his talk. I pushed my way through the throng of wet raincoats and clouds of cigarette smoke. On the dais Redgrove had survived the chairman's opening remarks and was in full flow.

'A tree in a storm is like a brain in a brain storm',' were the first words I heard. His voice was powerful with an actor's measured delivery, the pitch rising and falling like waves battering a passive shore. His poetry was full of images of raw energy at work in nature, rocks, water-wheels, rainbows and volcanic eruptions against a background of meditations on flowers and quotations from Wittgenstein. He was the perfect catalyst to my nascent creative self. He invited me to join the circle of artists, writers and sculptors which met in The Eldon, the university pub. The writer and critic Douglas Jefferson, an expert on Henry James was also an habitué but though he was on nodding terms with Redgrove, he had his own cronies. I bought all of Redgrove's books and went to his weekly creative writing class. Two other members of his class, Jon Glover and Jeffrey Wainbright, have subsequently become reasonably well-known writers and broadcaster. I hated both on sight and the feelings were mutual.

Redgrove was Gregory fellow for three years. In 1966 when Alan Tarling, who ran Poet and Printer Press, invited me to edit a pamphlet anthology of work by contemporary poets, I was delighted to include a selection of Redgrove's verse.

BT

ABOUT THE POET Peter Redgrove (1932 - 2003)

Peter William Redgrove was born on January 2, 1932 in Kingston-upon-Thames, Surrey. His parents were middle-class and Redgrove always had a difficult relationship with his father. After attending Taunton School in Somerset, he won a scholarship to study Natural Science at Queen's College, Cambridge. During a period of National Service in the Army, Redgrove was diagnosed as schizophrenic and given insulin shock treatment.

He left Cambridge in 1954 without a degree. But the experiences and friendships of Redgrove's undergraduate years remained very important. At Cambridge he joined Ted Hughes and Harry Guest in founding and editing the influential literary magazine *Delta*. He settled for a while in London, working as a copywriter and actively participating in a writers' group that included George MacBeth, Peter Porter and Martin Bell. He developed a close friendship in particular with the older Martin Bell. Redgrove also immersed himself in the works of C G Jung and Jungian psychology became a life-long inspiration.

With a Fulbright Fellowship, he was Visiting Poet at the University of Buffalo, New York, from 1961 to 1962. From 1962 to 1965 he succeeded his friend Jon Silkin as Gregory Fellow in Poetry at the University of Leeds. The university's special collections at its Brotherton Library hold Redtgrove's literary archives. From 1966 till his retirement in 1983 he was Poet and Lecturer at Falmouth School of Art, Cornwall. He was also a Visiting Professor at Colgate University, Hamilton, New York, from 1974 to 1975. Redgrove died in Falmouth on June 16, 2003.

Redgrove was an impressively prolific writer. His seven novels include two written with his second wife Penelope Shuttle. *In the Country of the Skin* (1973) deals with interchanging personalities. He also produced two collections of stories, numerous plays and radio and television plays, and edited or co-edited several poetry anthologies. One of his most important books was a collaboration with Penelope Suttle: *The Wise Wound* (1978), which was a revolutionary study of menstruation, almost a taboo subject at the time. But Redgrove's main legacy was his poetry. Over 35 collections were published in his lifetime.

Redgrove's many awards included: the Guardian Fiction Prize (1973), the Prudence Farmer Poetry Award (1977), the Cholmondley Award (1981), the Prix Italia (1982) and the prestigious Queen's Medal for Poetry (1996). He became a Fellow of the Royal Society of Literature in 1982 and received an honorary degree from the University of Sheffield in 2001.

Robin Robertson has commented that "Redgrove's poems electrify and astonish as they make us look again at our world – we come away changed." Peter Redgrove is a major twentieth century poet by any reckoning.

SELECT BIBLIOGRAPHY

POETRY COLLECTIONS

The Collector and Other Poems (Routledge, London, 1960).
At the White Monument and Other Poems (Routledge, 1963).
The God-Trap (Turret, London, 1966).
The Force and Other Poems (Routledge, 1966).
Penguin Modern Poets 11, with D. M. Black and D. M. Thomas. (Penguin, London, 1968).
The Mother, The Daughter and the Sighing Bridge (Sycamore Press, Oxford, 1970).
Love's Journeys (Second Aeon, Cardiff, 1971).
Loves Journeys: A Selection (Gilbertson, Crediton, Devon, 1971).
Dr. Faust's Sea-Spiral Spirit and Other Poems (Routledge, 1972).

The Hermaphrodite Album, with Penelope Shuttle(Fuller d'Arch Smith, London, 1973).
Sons of My Skin: Selected Poems 1954-1974, edited by Marie Peel (Routledge, 1975).
The Working of Water (Taxus Press, Durham, 1984)
In the Hall of the Saurians (Secker and Warburg, London, 1987).
My Father's Trapdoors (Jonathan Cape, London, 1994).
Selected Poems (Jonathan Cape, 1999).
From the Virgil Caverns (Jonathan Cape, 2002).
Sheen (Stride, 2003).

OTHER

Editor, with John Fuller and Harold Pinter, *New Poems 1967* (Hutchinson, London, 1968).
In the Country of the Skin (Sceptre Press, Rushden, 1972).
The Terrors of Dr Treviles, with Penelope Shuttle (Routledge, London, 1974).
Miss Carstairs Dressed for Blooding and Other Plays (Boyars, London, 1976).
The Hypnotist (play produced in Plymouth, 1978).
The Wise Wound:Menstruation and Everywoman, with Penelope Shuttle (Gollancz, London, 1978).
The God of Glass (Routledge, 1979).
Editor, with Jon Silkin, *New Poetry 5* (Hutchinson, 1979).
The Beekeepers (Routledge, 1980).
Editor, *Cornwall in Verse* (Secker and Warburg, 1982).
The Scientists of the Strange (radio play, 1984).
The Black Goddess and the Sixth Sense (Bloomsbury, London, 1987).
The One Who Set Out to Study Fear (Bloomsbury, 1989).

DC

POEMS BY PETER REDGROVE

Expectant Father

Final things walk home with me through Chiswick Park,
Too much death, disaster; this year
All the children play at cripples
And cough along with one foot in the gutter.
But now my staircase is a way to bed
And not the weary gulf she sprinted down for doorbells
So far gone on with the child a-thump inside;
A buffet through the air from the kitchen door that sticks
Awakes a thumb-size fly. Butting the rebutting window-pane
It shouts its buzz, so I fling the glass up, let it fly
Remembering as it skims to trees, too late to swat,
That flies are polio-whiskered to the brows
With breeding-muck, and home
On one per cent of everybody's children.

So it is the week when Matron curfews, with her cuffs,
And I draw back. My wife, round as a bell in bed, is white
 and happy.
Left to myself I undress for the night
By the fine bright wires of lamps: hot tips
To burrowing cables, the bloodscheme of the house,
Where flame sleeps. That,
With a shallow on the mattress from last night
Is enough to set me thinking on fired bones
And body-prints in the charcoal of a house, how
Darkness stands for death, and how afraid of sleep I am;
And fearing thus, thus I fall fast asleep.

But at six o'clock, the phone rings in – success!
The Sister tells me our son came up with the sun:
It's a joke she's pleased to make, and so am I.
I see out of the window it's about a quarter high,
And promises another glorious day.

A Storm

Somebody is throttling that tree
By the way it's threshing about;
I'm glad it's no one I know, or me,
The head thrust back at the throat,

Green hair tumbled and cracking throat.
His thumbs drive into her windpipe,
She cannot cry out,
Only swishing and groaning: death swells ripe,

The light is dimming but the fight goes on.
Chips strike my window. In the morning, there
Stands the tree, still, bushy and calm,
Not as I saw it, twisted heel to ear,

But fluffed up, boughs chafing slightly.
What's become of her attacker?
I'm glad he's not mine or known to me,
Flipped to the ground, heel over ear:

She preens herself, with a soft bough-purr.
Was he swallowed up, lip over ear?
He's gone anyway. The path is thick in her fur.

For No Good Reason

I walk on the waste-ground for no good reason
Except that fallen stones and cracks
Bulging with weed suit my mood
Which is gloomy, irascible, selfish, among the split timbers
Of somebody's home, and the bleached rags of wallpaper.
My trouser-legs pied with water-drops,
I knock a sparkling rain from hemlock-polls,
I crash a puddle up my shin,
Brush a nettle across my hand,
And swear – then sweat from what I said:
Indeed, the sun withdraws as if I stung.
Indeed, she withdrew as if I stung,
And I walk up and down among these canted beams,
        bricks and scraps,
Bitten walls and weed-stuffed gaps
Looking as it would feel now, if I walked back,
Across the carpets of my home, my own home.

Lazarus and the Sea

The tide of my death came whispering like this
Soiling my body with its tireless voice.
I scented the antique moistures when they sharpened
The air of my room, made the rough wood of my bed, (most dear),
Standing out like roots in my tall grave.
They slopped in my mouth and entered my plaited blood
Quietened my jolting breath with a soft argument
Of such measured insistence, untied the great knot of my heart.

They spread like whispered conversations
Through all the numbed rippling tissues radiated
Like a tree for thirty years from the still centre
Of my salt ovum. But this calm dissolution
Came after my agreement to the necessity of it;
Where before it was a storm over red fields
Pocked with the rain and the wheat furrowed
With wind, then it was the drifting of smoke
From a fire of the wood, damp with sweat,
Fallen in the storm.

I could say nothing of where I had been,
But I knew the soil in my limbs and the rain-water
In my mouth, knew the ground as a slow sea unstable
Like clouds and tolerating no organisation such as mine
In its throat of my grave. The knotted roots
Would have entered my nostrils and held me
By the armpits, woven a blanket for my cold body
Dead in the smell of wet earth, and raised me to the sky
For the sun in the slow dance of the seasons.
Many gods like me would be laid in the ground
Dissolve and be formed again in this pure night
Among the blessing of birds and the sifting water.
But where was the boatman and his gliding punt?
The judgment and the flames? These happenings
Were much spoken of in my childhood and the legends.
And what judgment tore me to life, uprooted me
Back to my old problems and to the family,
Charged me with unfitness for this holy simplicity.

Old House

I lay in an agony of imagination as the wind
Limped up the stairs and puffed on the landings,
Snuffled through floorboards from the foundations,
Tottered, withdrew into flaws, and shook the house.
Peppery dust swarmed through all cracks,
The boiling air blew a dry spume from other mouth;
From other hides and function:
Scale of dead people fountained to the ceiling—
What sort of a house is this to bring children to,

Bum it down, build with new-fired brick;
How many times has this place been wound up
Around the offensive memories of a dead person,
Or a palette of sick colours dry on the body,
Or bare arms through a dank trapdoor to shut off water
Or windows filmed over the white faces of children:
This is no place to bring children to"

I cried in a nightmare of more
Creatures shelled in bone-white,
Or dead eyes fronting soft ermine faces,
Or mantled in carnation, dying kings of creation, -
Or crimson mouth-skirts flashing as they pass-
What a world to bring new lives into,
Flat on my back in a warm bed as the house around me
Lived in the wind more than the people that built it;
It was bought with all our earned money,
With all the dust I was nearly flying from my body
That whipped in the wind in this normal November,
And outstretched beside her in my silly agony

She turned in her sleep and called for me,
Then taught me what children were to make a home for.

Anniversaire Triste

A piano plays my aunt in a lacquered room;
The wood and ivory lend a dead man sound;
Grinning with grilles, Samurai armour stands
Booming a little with the afterlife.

Her elbows stick out and her face goes down:
This is the climax, the triumphant foe
Death; I remember one tear really flew
And hit a vased rose, and hung there like a dew.

Indeed we all cried: herself, myself, the maid
Called in to listen to it once a year;
Her face came up, her fingers down! She was finished now
Labouring to communicate her pain.

She succeeded when she beat me stealing jam.
I found her piano-plaining pleasant, I'm afraid –
My boy's heart was carving with a penknife
A name, a heart, while sap oozed round the blade.

Nothing but Poking

Those stamens bang like a pouch.
From what dimension of colour
Sea of formal patterning and sex
They poke their privy tongues about
In a public garden on Sunday.
They ought to be stopped, they're that rude.
Then I saw a spurt of seed
Dash past in yellow breeze, disgraceful,
Every one rubbing. They are everywhere
Like a pumping up of spirit, an omnipresence,
Flowers chill the sunlight.

Insulted, they put the sun away
By which they are seen.
It slides like a liner out to sea
Skimming the earth, a great wake of clouds.
We all tip backwards into gazing darkness.
Now the flowers will not be visible
Not until they've finished, then
The sun will rise in repleted colours.

Jon Silkin

(1930 – 1997)

JOHN SILKIN

Jon Silkin I knew well as I attended a course in creative writing he ran under the auspices of Leeds University's Extra Mural Department. Silkin had just gained a First in English and was starting a doctoral thesis on the First World War poets which was never to be finished. Eventually he published the research in book-form. Silkin was short, stocky and immensely bearded. He was a Marxist of the most simplistic kind, but his doctrinaire socialism never appealed to me. He was distantly related to Jon Silkin QC, the scion of a politically powerful family and had in fact been educated at Dulwich College. His early poems had a powerful lyrical quality:

Searching how to relieve
The piled cacophony of
My spiritual unrest, I
Mistward that morning went

('The Area of Conflict' from *Re-ordering of the Stones*, Chatto; but Bryan should attack first.

When his spiritual gifts dried up he wrote political poems that I found dry and unattractive. Eventually Silkin settled permanently in Newcastle with a grant from the Arts Council to edit *Stand*, the magazine he founded. Occasionally I encountered him at readings and we smiled distantly at each other. We seemed to share a joke without quite knowing what it was.

BT

ABOUT THE POET Jon Silkin (1930 - 1997)

Jon Silkin was born in London on December 2, 1930, in a well-known Jewish family. One of his uncles was later to become a Labour peer. Silkin's life was characterised by restless travel and he later described himself as having the European Jew's 'rootless cosmopolitanism'. He had a chequered education and was expelled from Dulwich College, after which there was a stint in National Service in the Army Education Corp. Silkin also worked for six years in a succession of manual jobs, but also managed to bring out his first poetry collection, *A Portrait and Other Poems* in 1950.

In 1962 while working as a lavatory cleaner for an American firm in London, Silkin tried to organise a union of janitors to protest an employers' decision that they work overtime at the ordinary rate. This resulted in his dismissal; and Silkin invested the modest extra pay, received at the time of departure, in buying stationary to produce 400 copies of a mimeographed magazine that he then set about selling in coffee-bars. Thus was founded the well-known literary magazine, *Stand*. Except for a short break in 1957, Silkin was to run *Stand* for the rest of his life, and, as editor, he was committed to publish unfashionable and radical voices alongside mainstream ones.

The University of Leeds appointed Silkin as Gregory Fellow in Poetry from 1958 to 1960. This began a long love affair with the north. In 1960 some Leeds and Bradford businessmen helped him to revive *Stand* and, together with Andrew Gurr, Silkin established Northern House Pamphlet Poets. Silkin took his BA degree from Leeds in just two years in 1962, and from 1994 he served as Senior Fellow in Poetry at the same department where he had been a student. The following year the University's Brotherton Collection acquired the archives of *Stand*

From 1964 he made his home in Newcastle on Tyne and it was here that he died on November 24, 1997.

Jon Silkin's best-known poetry collection was *The Peaceable Kingdom* (1954) and his collection *Nature with Man* (1965) won the Faber Memorial Prize. His *Selected Poems* were published in 1980 and 1988. Always interested in war poetry, Silkin edited *The Penguin Book of First World War Poetry* (1979), *Wilfred Owen: The War Poems* (1994) and, with Jon Glover, *The Penguin Book of First World War Prose* (Penguin, 1989).
Fond of travelling, Silkin undertook several poetry readings in the USA in the 1960s and was a visiting writer in the USA, Australia, Israel, Korea and Japan. He was awarded the C. Day Lewis Fellowship in 1976-77 and was elected a Fellow of the Royal Society of Literature in 1986.

John Barnard has said: 'Jon Silkin will be remembered as a powerful and varied poetic voice and as a fierce and determined supporter of writers and writing.' In an obituary tribute published in *Stand*, Rodney Pybus wrote that: 'Jon Silkin, poet, editor and critic, is, quite simply, irreplaceable.'

SELECT BIBLIOGRAPHY

POETRY COLLECTIONS

Selected Poems (Routledge and Kegan Paul, London, 1980).
The Psalms and their Spoils (Routledge and Kegan Paul, 1980).
The Ship's Pasture.(Routledge and Kegan Paul, 1986).
The Lens-Breakers (Sinclair-Stevenson, London, 1992).
Selected Poems (Sinclair-Stevenson, 1993).
Watersmeet (The Bay Press, Whitley Bay, 1994).
Testament Without Breath, Images by Robert McNab. (Cargo Press, Cornwall, 1998).
Making a Republic (Carcanet / Northern House, 2002.

OTHER

Translator,.*Against Parting* by Natan Zach (Northern House Pamphlet Poets, 1967).

Out of Battle: The Poetry of the Great War London: (Oxford University Press, 1972).

Editor, *Poetry of the Committed Individual: A 'Stand' Anthology of Poetry* (Gollancz, London, 1973).

Editor, *The Penguin Book of First World War Poetry* (Penguin, 1979).

Gurney: A Play (Iron Press Drama Editions, Tyne & Wear, 1985).

Editor, with Jon Glover, *The Penguin Book of First World War Prose*. (Penguin, 1989).

Editor, *Wilfred Owen: The War Poems* (Sinclair-Stevenson, London, 1994)

The Life of Metrical & Free Verse in Twentieth-Century Poetry (Macmillans, London, 1997).

DC

POEMS BY JON SILKIN

A Daisy

Look unoriginal
Being numerous. They ask for attention
With that gradated yellow swelling
Of oily stamens. Petals focus them:
The eye-lashes grow wide.
Why should not one bring these to a funeral?
And at night, like children,
Without anxiety, their consciousness
Shut with white petals;

Blithe, individual.

The unwearying, small sunflower
Fills the grass
With versions of one eye.
A strength in the full look
Candid, solid, glad.
Domestic as milk.

In multitudes, wait,
Each, to be looked at, spoken to.
They do not wither;
Their going, a pressure
Of elate sympathy
Released from you.
Rich up to the last interval
With minute tubes of oil, pollen;
Utterly without scent, for the eye,

For the eye, simply. For the mind
And its invisible organ,
That feeling thing.

Durham bread

Streets of terrace houses cover
the hill, the sun's tufts and hollows
in lilac smoke turning the stone
to honey. The railway steps
through on arches. This is Gala
miner and minister, bands that break
lugubrious cries. The hushed brass,
its softly hurled quick touches
a friend's death: yes, I loved you.

Living, like smoke
on stone property, patches of brick
darn a worn fabric, its patch
of small-builders. With stepping
between, a miner,
a lawyer, fragrant and striped
as a cardamom. A tall bird
uncurls its neck
and rises like a figure
off a tarnished penny.
Its streaks of bodily black force
drift at the dun stone
of church architecture.

Some choose not to have
that church. Christ so imbues them,
these workers in Frosterly marble,
their fossil columns, they drop
their Christianity
in heaps of languid clothing
on the river side, swimming until
their bodies with tiredness fill,
naked as the soft opening
they started through.

Walking, what I see,
the air lifting between the stepping arches,
its how their spaces
are like the thick slices of Durham bread, cut
against hunger,
slices like generations of boys' mouths,
this boy, Dick, even
now, cramming his
with white, thick unbuttered bread. He feels
that bub, that generative, pert
tenderness of his wife's breasts. His hands
echo her shapes. Durham

bread, as the trains wing it, where
some have neither bread nor love. Slovenly
clothes crease the frail height
of a man buying his stamp,
whose monarch's head removes
a letter to his friend. Take the bread.

To My Friends

It does not matter she never knew
Who Pater was. What is rare
Despite the encirclements of marriage
Or even the political relationships
Affianced beyond parliament
Is love, which breaks the breads.
The staff of women, the dread,
The hunger of men, it is not
Just what I am capable of
If mature; it is the force
Behind those intimations of our senses
progenitor to morc growth,
If anything is. Remember,
The moulds of rock perish,
The flower so delicately formed
The minute exactness seems meant
To last. What does live
In the complex fabrics of air,
Uncoloured, and always nubile,
Is this man-like attribute.
So very carefully
Consider what you do
As an action related always
To this eternal motion
In man's leathery breast;
For the way we treat each other
In private is, minutely,
The way we deal with wives
And they their men. Even stones
Wrinkled in a contempt

Of their manipulators
Lie in some comradeship,
For their sakes. And for Man,
Men matter, whether that God
Who made us, and the stones,
Is watching us, or bored
With human agony
Lies in immortal sleep
Terribly locked, not witnessing
The outrages of human hunger
Bearable only because
They must be, even these uptorn
Grains of love that are burned
In complex and primitive agonies
In concentration camps.

Caring for Animals

I ask sometimes why these small animals
With bitter eyes, why we should care for them.

I question the sky, the serene blue water,
But it cannot say. It gives no answer.

And no answer releases in my head
A procession of grey shades patching and whimpering;

Dogs with clipped ears, wheezing cart horses,
A fly without shadow and without thought.

Is it with these menaces to our vision
With this procession led by a man carrying wood

We must be concerned? The holy land, the rearing
Green island should be kindlier than this.

Yet the animals, our ghosts, need tending to.
Take in the whipped cat and the blinded owl;

Take up the man-trapped squirrel upon your shoulder.
Attend to the unnecessary beasts.

From growing mercy and a moderate love
Great love for the human animal occurs.

And your love grows. Your great love grows and grows.

The Ship's Pasture

In the sun, the leaf, hesitant but active
this florescence of plain wood; with joy
I saw the fields of England, as new, chartered
shapes, bargained for, and so, snipped
with standing sheep, their snowy garments
by the limestone walls, bulbous fossils,
their thick inert forms braids dangling
the soft wealth of England: Selah. Except
some people here are brutal, the fist,
because of standing in the wrong place,
at the cheekbone. Fist, or snide
arrowy word.

I rose from England much refreshed, but returned
at evening; much undone that was once good
prior to this mean juncture. It was joy,
beside my self, to see the new fields. Whose
is this land that, like waiting flesh, turns
with a kiss, domestic, but yet is
a local habitation with no substance or name
sustaining it? It is a ship's pasture,
its interlinking husk submarine,
sea-spike, the sleeted fields of destruction:
for payment, for emolument. I am
a part of this—the bee, cutter of wood,
whose timbered house is unimaginably
hospitable. This is what it is. Northwards,
a new Jerusalem with the lamb lies separate,
its shade dense and lovely. The woman
starts again, as if each portion of this
were knit afresh.

Bill Turner

(b. 1927)

ABOUT THE POET Bill Turner (b. 1927)

William Price Turner was born in York on 14th August 1927. He was educated at Whitehill Secondary School in Glasgow and did his military service in the Royal Engineers from 1945 to 1947. He married Anne Hamilton Hill in 1950 and they had two children.

From 1951 to 1956 he was Editor of *The Poet* in Glasgow, and from 1957 to 1960 he worked for the BBC in Glasgow as Television Captions Artist and Assistant Floor Manager. He wrote several radio plays during this time.

Turner settled in Leeds in 1960 when he was awarded a Gregory Fellowship at the University. The university's Brotherton Library contains an autographed manuscript of one of his poems. From 1962 to 1963 he became Sub-Editor of the *Yorkshire Post*, and then the newspaper's Crime Fiction Reviewer until 1966. From 1963 to 1966 he also served as a Tutor in Creative Writing at Swarthmore Adult Education Centre in Leeds. A Scottish Arts Council Award in 1970 came as a welcome recognition of his writing. The University of Glasgow appointed Turner as a Creative Writing Fellow from 1973 to 1975.

An eclectic writer, Turner has turned his hand to different genres of writing. His early novels were written under the name Bill Turner and include *Bound to Die* (1967), *Sex Trap* (1968) and *Circle of Squares* (1969). Later novels like *Soldier's Woman* (1972) and *Hot-Foot* (1973) used the name William Turner. A libretto, *Baldy Bane*, was written for the BBC in London in 1967. But Turner's biggest output is his poetry. His first collection, *First Offence*, was published in 1954. Like his prose, Turner's poetry too was sometimes published under the name William Turner and he also used the name W Price Turner, but on the whole he preferred to be known as Bill Turner.

BIBLIOGRAPHY

POETRY COLLECTIONS

First Offence (Derek Maggs, Bristol, 1954).
The Rudiment of an Eye (Villiers, London, 1955).
The Flying Corset (Villiers, 1962).
Fables from Life (Northern House, Newcastle upon Tyne, 1966).
More Fables from Life (Ulsterman, Belfast, 1969).
The Moral Rocking-Horse (Barrie and Jenkins, London, 1970).

OTHER

Bound to Die (Constable, London, 1967).
Sex Trap (Constable, 1968).
Circle of Squares (Constable, London, 1967).
Another Little Death (Constable, London, 1967).
Soldier's Woman (Constable, London, 1967).
Hot-Foot (Constable, London, 1967).

DC

POEMS BY BILL TURNER

A Tramp Looks Back

She sees me pass her window and she smiles
although she knows I go to no safe bed,
but there's a kind of blessing in her eyes
that cancels all the tumult in my head
the way the moon stays through a brawl of clouds
and stares until the sky is clean and clear.
I feel her wish me well, and then I seem
to will my rags and years to disappear . . .
Was I a pilgrim once, and she a queen?
Was she a prisoner, and I a knight?
She saw me pass her window and she smiled,
and death shrank back from that enduring light.
I have forgotten the battles and the scars,
but I remember her both cool and warm.
We gave each other comfort in duress;
we shared a still place in the howling storm.
Was it in reeds I hid, or else in oaks?
No matter. That was centuries ago.
As wheels go round we cannot count the spokes.
Good night, sweet lady whom I used to know.

Homely Accommodation, Suit Gent

In that repository of auction pots and post-Ark
furniture, stepping over the creaking board
you always sprang another, setting Mrs. Hagglebroth

ready to intercept you with her pleated smile
and plucked eyebrows up, while conducting her
wallpaper centenary festival with a stick of feathers.

In that saddlesoap atmosphere, there was no music
after Mozart, and no smoking in the dining-room.
Sunlight was discouraged: it fades the draperies.
Sunday papers she detested, like all dirt. Even
the bought earth was sterilised before the bulbs,
one to a tub, were planted; God rest their souls.

But the remarkable strain of slaughterhouse fly
that bloated its dipstick in her best insecticide
always escaped her notice, though she stiffened
at irregular movements of bedsprings, and blushed
when the cistern gargled openly. Somehow her gentlemen
kept moving on, though she prayed for them all.

It was as if, when the seed stirred in them, they
thought of her with rubber gloves on, oiling her shears
and fled, a week overpaid. Behind her back, when
she went to church, talk about warthogs in war-togs,
they called her Brothelhag, bartering sniggers,
and the sweat chilled on them in case she knew.

One lay awake at night sheeted in terror, when
the Hagglebroth bloomers billowing from the line
rose in binocular glory and loomed at his window
like a zeppelin. He left. They all left. Even
the glutted fly. Finally Mrs. Hagglebroth herself
left, in a brand-new box, sealed against sunlight.
So we have here the Hagglebroth effects. The souls
of miscellaneous gentlemen, welded to wicker chairs.

The fears of young men and the dread of old, potted
in antique brass. Several conscience racks, disguised
as beds. Connoisseur stuff, all of it. So come now
ladies, you have your catalogues. What am I bid?

The Third Culture

At the Universities' Poetry Conference
I sat and glowered at the platform array,
seated like prize potted plants in their gay
and studied cool indifference
to whatever the outside crops suffer of weather.
And I wished I had never come away
from the cultivation of my own garden,
however wrong the soil may be for heather,
for I thought I heard a fat slug beg my pardon
that his prosperity was owing to King Weed.
We all knew it, but those sensitive tendrils curled
at the simple tribute, and the glad feelers indeed
wagged moistly that they should be on the same
wave-length so often. It is the way of the world
that weeds and insects grab bounty beyond their need.
They say you can't fight it; you must join the Game.
But while a bud can bloom, I call it appalling
that the good sweet earth be choked to this extent
and the summit of summer robbed of decent scent
with under the surface all that greedy crawling.

Rose Harem

A black cat, warily decanting itself
from a low wall outside
a house almost hidden by roses,
suspends its flow as if I had said 'When.'
The trick with cats is to out-ignore
them. I have seen cats enough
before, anyway, but roses like these
heavy-headed brutes, pale lemon,
salmon, red, never outside
an exhibition tent, and then
usually over shoulders. There's one
with a pink core and orange ruff
that's crazed with crimson veins.
And farther back – excuse me, cat –
a nodding beauty, honey-gold,
like the expensive skin of an
unspanked princess. Gardens like this –
you *bore* me, cat – ought to be kept in
trust for tawny naked girls
and undomesticated animals,
so probably it belongs to some
wrinkled witch whose – all *right*, then,
one caress. Yes, you're a black velvet
rose of cats, a furry prize, but …
Blooming villain! Keep your thorns to yourself.
I might have guessed. I'm going now. Look
who's aloof again. Back on his brick
shelf, in charge: sleek custodian
of sweetly purring roses. So long,
sentinel. My compliments to your

fluttering arch-conspirators; they put on
a good show, quite a tease ... And it's not
every day a man gets solicited by
an imperial pimp alert for wayward bees.

Progress Report

The future isn't what is used to be.
What if the past turns out to be a fake.
Sometimes we have to close our eyes to see
meanings that disappear before we wake.
In childhood it took chalk marks against doors
to prove the growth another year had seen.
When was it that we first found subtler chores
to track the spirit by, and keep it keen?
Perception's rings are safe within scarred bark.
How many insights add up to one notch?
The age of flint evokes a leaping spark,
and the scent of roses can stop a watch.

Inheritance

My father was a man of charity:
the bookies and tobacco barons
blessed his regular donations.
He was a man of great faith
in all racing tipsters
and in the divine

rightness of Dad.
Now my two sons,
taking for granted
books, records, cameras:
things I never owned before
I earned them myself, pine among
the sad litter of their possessions
for new goods; my values are meaningless.
I thank my father for this generous
hole bequeathed me for my belt: I use
no other. To my sons I leave
freedom to choose their vices.
But which is the greater
shame, admitting your
dad's a poet
or your own son?
I'd like to have spared
all three of you such pains
of embarrassment over
this one talent you'd each rather
have buried, but to prosper it must
be shared, gain interest, and be passed on.

Keeping Up Appearances

When there's no moonlight to silver the crocuses
in the darkness of the park, one focuses

on a pale semblance of frost that lies
approximately where our cheated eyes

believe that daylight blue and gold exist.
The unrealities of love persist.

On this mild night we walk hand-in-hand,
certain of our path, although we understand

little of these blind forces we are prepared
to trust: the fleshly splendours we have shared,

the mazes of the mind, are cloudy stuff.
For the time being, we have said enough.

Leaning on railings, by the hidden lake,
we recall paths we did not take

while an owl questions us. A shaggy dog pauses
to ponder our imponderable causes

and passes on to more substantial scents.
The realities of love and its events

are lowly, but may loom exceeding large
for those with obligations to discharge.

David Wright

(1920 – 1994)

DAVID WRIGHT

The deaf poet David Wright followed Peter Redgrove as Gregory Fellow in Leeds. He belonged to an older and more cosmopolitan group than Redgrove. He had known Dylan Thomas and belonged to the circle of George Barker and David Gascoygne, whose publisher had been David Archer's Parton Press.

Just before meeting Wright I wrote a review of an anthology of contemporary verse he had edited for Penguin. The book was full of the work of his friends and I wrote a blistering review that was published in *Peace News*. Fortunately the review escaped Wright's notice.

As a person, he was kindness itself but his ideas about poetry seemed very dull. He knew hundreds of anecdotes about the private lives of poets with which he regaled the student literati of Leeds University.

When I became immersed in poetry, the Leeds City Library bought all the latest collections as they came out and I developed an encyclopaedic knowledge of contemporary English and American poetry in the sixties. Ever ready to encourage others, David Wright was kind enough to say that I had a better working knowledge of new poetry than anyone he had known in London.

BT

ABOUT THE POET David Wright (b. 1920-1994)

David John Murray Wright was born in Johannesburg, South Africa, in 1920. He became deaf in childhood and, at the age of fourteen, came to England to study at Northampton School for the Deaf and later at Oriel College, Oxford. He later wrote the autobiographical *Deafness: A Personal Account* (1969).

After graduating in 1942, he worked for *The Sunday Times* for five years. In 1947 he became a freelance writer. He wrote a critical book, *Roy Campbell*, about the work of a South African compatriot. Jointly with his friend Patrick Swift, he founded and edited the literary quarterly *X* from 1959 to 1962. Also with Swift, he wrote three books about Portugal. With another literary friend, John Heath-Stubbs, he co-edited *The Faber Book of Twentieth Century Verse* (Faber & Faber, London 1975). As an anthologist, he is known especially for his Penguin collections, including *The Penguin Book of English Romantic Verse* (1968). In this connection, it may be observed that in adult life, the South African poet loved to live in the Lake District.

It is David Wright's own sensitive and intelligent verse that will survive the test of time. He has left such impressive collections as *Monologue of a Deaf Man* (1958), *To the Gods the Shades: New and Collected Poems* (1976), *Selected Poems* (1988) and *Elegies* (1990).

Writing about his poetry in *The Oxford Companion to Twentieth-Century Poetry*, T J G Harris has commented that: "it creates the lively curve of an eminently humane mind's thinking and speaking".

BIBLIOGRAPHY

POETRY COLLECTIONS

Moral Stories (Verschoyle, London, 1954).
Monologue of a Deaf Man (A Deutsch, London, 1958).
Adam at Evening (Hodder & Stoughton, London, 1965).
To the Gods the Shades: New and Collected Poems (Carcanet, Manchester, 1976).
Selected Poems (Carcanet, Manchester, 1988).
Elegies (Greville, Warwick, 1990).
Poems and Versions (Carcanet, 1992).

OTHER

Deafness: A Personal Account (1969). Later published as *Deafness: An Autobiography* (Mandarin, 1993).
Roy Campbell (Longman, London, 1961).
Editor, *Seven Victorian Poets* (Heinemann, London, 1964).
Editor, *The Mid-century: English Poetry 1940-60* (Penguin, London, 1965).
Editor, *Longer Contemporary Poems* (1966).
Editor, *The Penguin Book of English Romantic Verse* (Penguin, London, 1968).
Co-editor with John Heath-Stubbs, *The Faber Book of Twentieth Century Verse* (Faber & Faber, London, 1975).
Editor, *Penguin Book of Everyday Verse* (Penguin, 1976).

DC

POEMS BY DAVID WRIGHT

To John Heath-Stubbs

My half-blind friend, whom solitary as a crane I first saw awkwardly
run
On pavements out of his element, as if behind his sky-scraper
back there shone
Glances of Eumenides invisible to everyone but to him; whom I have
seen take
Real flight on wings that in the sky seem easy and slack,
I dedicate to him, to this his quarrel and continual love
Of liberty and verse, this verse: to testify of
The gifts he has kept from a bag of money. May his Muse to him
Bend, bend to her lover reading the leaves in a forest of autumn,
Where, overhead, migratory birds are flying, singing, flying and
singing.

A Visit to a Poet

Recently I went to visit a poet in jail
(A place which in two ways reminded me of hell,
Being both hygienic and a dominion
Where everyone's responsibility has gone),
One who, justly imprisoned for injuring the State
By not joining the Army, preferring to try to write
Verses unlikely to sell, in abnormally good
Health, a new suit of clothes, and with regular food,
Cut off from supplies of harmful alcoholic drink,
With paper and pen, with a room, and with time to think,
Everything, in fact, unnecessary to the Muse,
Suffers barren confinement on the outskirts of Lewes.

Elegy

In memoriam M H M

Put seventy years of no
Wit or beauty in the grave,
These folded hands that have
Given love that cannot go
Further than divinity,
Fold on her virginity.
We have seen death invade
Auchlewan glens. Death like our
Dying power slowly burns
Lowland mountains, greens of Barr,
And the rowans hirpling down
The spate of Stinchar. Turn
The locked mill. Pinclanty, on your
Axle of poverty and song;
The learned and bloody hills of Ayr
Cover their heads with autumn.
Back to Scotland with these bones,
And to Dumfriesshire her daughter,
Where the Annan water foils
The red boulders of too great
Pride. The flood to Solway bears
Blood of Scotland to the flinching
Stallions whose beating hair
Dries on Ailsa, whips upon
The arm of Jura. As her son,
As her son I stand beside
Her unmonumental stone;
As her son no passion
But of mourning for the beauty

Of the covenanted days
That her barren arms relinquish.
For her sons I stand beside
The dead ground that shall receive her,
For her sons that in the seven
Miracles of heaven stand,
Turning grief and love toward her.
Margaret Murray was her name.

An Invocation to the Goddess

O sea born and obscene
Venus I see ascend
Fishbright upon a shell
Out of a salty pool
Angels and flesh attend,
The dolphin-sewn and blown
Mirrors of sea surround
As bawdy as a boy
That blank desirous form.
The goddess smiles from joy,
I look her in the groin;
Her seakale coloured eyes
Acknowledge her concern.
Not the ideal but real
Half sheltered by her hand,
Sty of ambiguities
Offensive and divine.
Venus preferring joy
Defenceless from the sea
Attending to defend,

Feminine, debonair,
Step naked to the shore.
Step, wound in your hair,
And singing galleries
Fish, fowl, flesh, surround you.
I cry your worshipper
Upon this island ground
Down by a sky and still
Crying borne by a sea,
Rejected and acclaimed.
Announce perfection, smile
Upon what is deformed,
Accept what is, and be.

An Apology to the Dead

I was conceived in the Llanstephan Castle
Sliding like a swan on a careless ocean
With hardly a ripple, and my home should be
Among leagues and legions of that sea,
Rather than on the island where I am
Surrounded by silence, and my grandfather's home
Alone to the wind listens with one tenant only
As autumn continually falls around.
Like the Neapolitan king Ariel drowned
In a prince's ear, I feel a change
Turning my bones. I turn to and from
My ancestors, for I will not be one
Among them on the ocean's either side,
Whose froth and bubble I make my bride.

A Funeral Oration

Composed at thirty, my funeral oration: Here lies
David John Murray Wright, 6’2”, myopic blue eyes;
Hair grey (very distinguished looking, so I am told);
Shabbily dressed as a rule; susceptible to cold;
Acquainted with what are known as the normal vices;
Perpetually short of cash; useless in a crisis;
Preferring cats, hated dogs; drank (when he could) too much;
Was deaf as a tombstone; and extremely hard to touch.
Academic achievements: BA, Oxon (2nd class);
Poetic: the publication of one volume of verse,
Which in his thirtieth year attained him no fame at all
Except among intractable poets, and a small
Lunatic fringe congregating in Soho pubs.
He could roll himself cigarettes from discarded stubs,
Assume the first position of Yoga; sail, row, swim;
And though deaf, in church appear to be joining a hymn.
Often arrested for being without a permit,
Starved on his talents as much as he dined on his wit,
Born in a dominion to which he hoped not to go back
Since predisposed to imagine white possibly black:
His life, like his times, was appalling; his conduct odd;
He hoped to write one good line; died believing in God.

Monologue of a Deaf Man

Et lui comprit trop bien, n'ayant pas entendu.
– Tristan Corbière

It is a good plan, and began with childhood
As my fortune discovered, only to hear
How much it is necessary to have said.
Oh silence, independent of a stopped ear,
You observe birds, flying, sing with wings instead.

Then do you console yourself? You are consoled
If you are, as all are. So easy a youth
Still unconcerned with the concern of a world
Where, masked and legible, a moment of truth
Manifests what, gagged, a tongue should have told;

Still observer of vanity and courage
And of these mirror as well; that is something
More than a sound of violin to assuage
What the human being most dies of: boredom
Which makes hedgebirds clamour in their black thorn cage.

But did the brushless fox die of eloquence?
No, but talked himself, it seems, into a tale.
The injury, dominated, is an asset;
It is there for domination, that is all.
Else what must faith do deserted by mountains?

Talk to me then, you who have so much to say,
Spectator of the human conversation,
Reader of tongues, examiner of the eye,
And detective of clues in every action,
What could a voice, if you heard it, signify?

The tone speaks less than a twitch and a grimace.
People make to depart, do not say 'Goodbye'.
Decision, indecision, drawn on every face
As if they spoke. But what do they really say?
You are not spared, either, the banalities.

In whatever condition, whole, blind, dumb,
One-legged or leprous, the human being is,
I affirm the human condition is the same,
The heart half broken in ashes and in lies,
But sustained by the immensity of the divine.

Thus I too must praise out of a quiet ear
The great creation to which I owe I am
My grief and my love. O hear me if I cry
Among the din of birds deaf to their acclaim
Involved like them in the not unhearing air.

The Night of the Centenary of the Death of Emily Bronte

The two worlds that have attended her
Voice burn a candle. Time places the bow
Of a moon, virgin and huntress, over her
Grave, where today a century folds
On her a hundred leaves, and December
Rides on a hundred wings of snow.

Acknowledgements

The editors and publisher thank the following for permission to reprint the selections in this book.

Peter Porter for Martin Bell's 'Reasons for Refusal', 'Senilio Passes, Singing', 'A Benefit Night at the Opera', 'It Is the Blight Man Was Born For', 'A Prodigal Son for Volpone' and 'Prospect 1939', published in *Complete Poems* (Bloodaxe).

Julia Blackburn for her 'Introduction' and for Thomas Blackburn's 'The Younger Son', 'The Lucky Marriage', 'Oedipus', 'No Single Station', 'The Villain', 'Trewarmett' and 'A Small Keen Wind', published in *Selected Poems* edited by Julia Blackburn (Carcanet Press, 2001).

Wayne Brown for his 'Cat Poem', 'On the Coast', 'The Tourists', 'Sing Willow', 'Drought' and 'Light and Shade', published in *On the Coast* (André Deutsch).

Kevin Crossley-Holland for his 'A Dream of a Meeting', 'Dusk, Burnham-Overy-Staithe', 'Confessional', 'The Wall', 'A Lindisfarne Tombstone', 'Vision' and 'Woman Sorting Redcurrants', published in *Selected Poems* (Enitharmon Press).

John Heath-Stubbs for his 'The Timeless Nightingale', 'When Sappho Loved', 'A Cassida for Sadegh Hedayat', 'To Edmund Blunden', 'Good Night, Ireen', 'On the Demolition of the Odeon Cinema, Westbourne Grove', 'Titus and Berenice', 'Letter to David Wright', 'Casta Diva' and 'For David Gascoyne', published in *Collected Poems 1943-1987* (Carcanet Press).

Pearse Hutchinson for his 'Málaga', 'Gaeltacht', 'Wouldn't I?', 'A True Story Ending in False Hope', 'Look, No Hands', 'Amhrán na mBréag' and 'The Miracle of Bread and Fiddles', published in *Collected Poems* (Gallery Press).

James Kirkup for his 'The Love that Dares to Speak its Name', 'Emily in Winter', 'Summertime in Leeds', 'In a London Schoolroom', 'To an Old Lady Asleep at a Poetry Reading' and 'The Poet', published in *The Selected Shorter Poems* Vols. 1 & 2 (University of Salzburg).

Smith/Doorstop Press for Paul Mills' 'Brenda', 'The Common Talk', 'News From Nowhere', 'A Balinese Mask', 'Single Parent' and 'Christmas Day', published in *Dinosaur Point* (Smith/Doorstop Books).

David Higham Associates for Peter Redgrove's 'A Storm', 'Lazarus and the Sea', 'Old House' and 'Anniversaire Triste', published in *The Collector and Other Poems* (Routledge); 'Expectant Father' and 'For No Good Reason', published in *The Nature of Cold Weather and Other Poems* (Routledge); and 'Nothing but Poking', published in *The Force and Other Poems* (Routledge).

Sinclair-Stevenson for Jon Silkin's 'A Daisy', 'Durham Bread', 'To My Friends', 'Caring for Animals' and 'The Ship's Pasture', published in *Selected Poems* (Sinclair-Stevenson).

Barry Tebb for his biographical extracts, versions of which were previously published in his autobiography, *Dancing to Nobody's Tune* (Sixties Press), and for 'My James Kirkup', which was published in *Diversions* edited by James Hogg (University of Salzburg).

Barrie and Jenkins for Bill Turner's 'A Tramp Looks Back', 'Homely Accommodation, Suit Gent', 'Progress Report', 'Rose Harem', 'The Third Culture', 'Inheritance' and 'Keeping Up Appearances', published in *The Moral Rocking-Horse* (Barrie and Jenkins, London, 1970).

Carcanet Press for David Wright's 'To John Heath-Stubbs', 'A Visit to a Poet', 'Elegy', 'An Invocation to the Goddess', 'An Apology to the Dead', 'A Funeral Oration', 'Monologue of a Deaf Man' and 'The Night of the Centenary of the Death of Emily Bronte', published in *To the Gods the Shades: New and Collected Poems* (Carcanet Press, 1976).

* *